Haiti
The Lost Paradise

Haiti
The Lost Paradise

By Lynda Criswell

Haiti: The Lost Paradise

Cover photo by Jack R. Criswell

Back cover by Jack G. Criswell

Copyright © 2010 by Lynda Criswell

All rights reserved. No part of this book may be reproduced or transmitted in any form or by any means without written permission of the author.

All Bible references are to the King James Version.

ISBN 978-0-557-40567-1

Would you like to take a two-month visit with me to Milot, Haiti? This book is based on e-mails written in the process of setting up sewing and computer vocational schools under the authority of Good Shepherd Ministry. This trip, The Haiti Project, was sponsored through the generosity and support of friends and members of Glen Iris Baptist Church in Birmingham, Alabama.

The Haitian people I met have become tangled in my heart. I hope you will share my feelings through the words that God has given me to glorify Him.

Lynda Criswell

Prologue

This is a true story of God's work in the lives of His people. This journey began for me in July, 2008.

The members of Glen Iris Baptist Church in Birmingham, Alabama, were planning to go to Haiti for their annual mission trip. My husband Jack was planning to go. I was not.

Lamar Lyon, the American representative for Good Shepherd Ministry in Haiti, told me of their need for a sewing teacher to establish a vocational school. God communicated directly to my heart that this project was for me. He began filling my mind with ideas and techniques I could use. I could hardly sleep because of the anticipation.

I stood in my sewing room at home, recalling great memories of past students, and felt tears well up as I thanked God for this new blessing. I was humbled that God could have chosen so many more qualified people for this, yet He chose me.

Then He began to work.

By August, I was trying to figure out how to get a simple pattern in multiple sizes to use in teaching. Tissue patterns would not stand that much use, and it would be expensive to purchase one pattern for every student. My son Wes suggested I trace them on heavy plastic. But how could I possibly get that much plastic and trace all the pattern pieces in every size and cut them out quickly?

Wes's builder volunteered to donate the plastic.

On August 22, I thought it would be nice to get a serger for the missionary's wife, Sandy Younger. I told no one.

On August 23, Sharon from Glen Iris offered to buy a serger for Haiti.

Pastor Lamb announced that the ladies' meeting in September would trace and cut patterns for Haiti.

In September, I asked Mr. Lyon what he thought would motivate the students. His answer was, "Hope. And you are bringing it to them." Again, I experienced a personal confirmation and presence from God that was both overwhelming and humbling.

I began organizing the supplies to be put on the shipping container leaving from Florida in October. No one had donated trim or scissors. These items are usually plentiful around those who sew. I went to work the next morning and unlocked the door to find two boxes overflowing with trims donated to Haiti.

I went by a major department store after work to return an item and told the employees this story. Customers and employees gathered and listened. There were tears. One employee walked away. I was afraid I had offended her. She returned with thirty-six pairs of new scissors in a box. I asked her why the store had so many scissors. She replied: "Because you needed them."

I literally could not keep up with God's flow of blessings. Jack bought two big plastic tubs to hold the trims that I did not even have twenty-four hours earlier.

Someone donated a huge box of serger thread. Oops! I forgot to tell God I needed serger thread for the serger He supplied. He sent it anyway. He knows our needs, even if we do not.

The cleaners next door to the place where I work donated huge boxes of buttons.

My sister Margaret's church donated boxes of items, including a Singer Featherweight and a hem marker. I was reluctant to request a hem marker because so few people knew what one is. God knew we needed one and someone listened.

The members at Glen Iris Baptist Church in Birmingham, Alabama, donated sewing machines. One family donated a Singer 201–2, a virtual workhorse of a machine that had been used on the mission field by a relative of theirs. The missionary had died, but her estate had not been settled until now—just when there was a need.

A customer at the store where I work gave me a forty-dollar check for Haiti.

An upscale consignment store donated a sack full of jewelry I could use for rewards.

A single man at church opened his wallet. There were several one-dollar bills. He pulled out the only twenty-dollar bill and told me to use it for Haiti.

We realized we will need thirty tables and forty chairs. This was a huge financial obligation to us, but not to God. A relative of a church member arranged a big discount at a home improvement store. Glen Iris paid the bill with donations.

My living room and dining room were covered with boxes, bags, sacks, and containers full of items God's people had provided. Looking at the abundance filled me with humility and gratitude.

Someone donated a tailor's tack. It requires special carbon paper that I did not have. Marking pens do not work well in high humidity. Later that same day a dermatologist donated the carbon paper.

God was bringing everything in on His schedule. Only about two thousand dollars for our Missionary Flights International (MFI) airfare was left to pay. I wasn't worried. I knew I could write that check.

In late December I began to feel doubt and emotional pressure. I determined to rely on God to give me spirit "of power, and of love, and of a sound mind." (II Timothy 1:7) Almost immediately He created in me a sense of fulfillment and joy and praise. We have a God who is greater than he that is within the world. (1 John 4:4)

I got the malaria pills and tetanus shots, and completed my dental checkup the week before Christmas. It was a little early, but I felt compelled to get those chores out of the way.

That afternoon Jack and I went to Costco to buy a Christmas turkey. His company called him on his cell phone and gave him notice they were letting him go. We were stunned. Now I understood why I felt I should go ahead with the dental and doctor visits ahead of schedule. We now had neither insurance nor a paycheck to cover that looming airfare.

We returned the turkey.

Jack had been asked to start a computer school at the vocational school, but could not get that much time off from his job. It was as if God was telling us, "Oh? Is your job in the way of My work? I can take care of that."

Charlotte offered to buy us a Christmas turkey. My son Jack offered to take us out to eat.

Up until this time, I was happily working in my own power, thrilled to watch God bring in supplies to help me. Now I realized He was supplying what we needed out of His abundance. He did not need us or Jack's job. We needed Him.

Was God giving us more time to stay in Haiti? Was He testing us? Was Satan sending us problems to discourage us? I still trusted God. He has never failed me.

A man in our church who lives in a retirement home gave us one hundred and fifty dollars.

I took my car into the shop with a malfunction. The maintenance man and I were discussing his problems, and I told him about the Haiti Project. Then my car was ready. The manager said he had overheard what I told their maintenance man about the Haiti Project. There would be no charge for the work. This was their Christmas gift to me. Try that with your car dealer.

A customer who was a cancer survivor asked me if I knew of a cause she could support. I told her about Haiti. A customer waiting overheard and said he wanted to give, too.

A woman I had not seen in four years came to the store where I work. I told her about Haiti. She wrote me a check for three hundred dollars.

A church member silently passed me a one hundred-dollar bill.

One of my sewing students called and I told her about Haiti. She discussed it with her husband. He took up a collection at his gym.

In February, Pastor Lamb wrote the check that I could not write to cover our airfare to Good Shepherd Ministries (GSM). Donations had come in from people everywhere who were obedient to God's leading. God did not need our money. He owns it all already.

These are only a few of the miracles and coincidences that God arranged.

We serve a mighty God. I have learned that your life is not about you. It is about God.

Enjoy the journey.

The eyes of the Lord run to and fro throughout the whole earth to shew Himself strong in the behalf of those whose heart is perfect toward Him. (II Chronicles 16:9)

Some Important People

Adams, Mr. and Mrs.—friends and members of Glen Iris Baptist Church (GIB)
Aimee—Haitian girl living at mission
AuRel—GSM devotion member and friend
BeBe—GSM employee and friend
Beth—GIB member and friend
Charlotte—GIB member and friend
Criswell family:
Jack—husband
Lynda—wife and author
    Jack and Cynthia—son and his wife
        Cara and Schaeffer—their children
    Wes and Kristy—son and his wife
        Wesley and Kristy—grandson and his wife
Christian—GSM supervisor
FiFi—Haitian versatile interpreter
Guy—GSM grammar school principal and fashion show emcee
Dorothy—author of Haitian language book, missionary, and friend
Gourneau—administrator of all GSM schools
Hilaire—GSM high school French teacher and music director
Inno—GSM employee and Nezzie's helper
James—GSM school secretary and son of Nezzie
Joscelyn—GSM employee and friend
Johny—GSM biology teacher
Brother Jonathan—GIB's ten-talented music director
Ken and Sophia—GIB members and friends
Lamar—GSM employee and friend
Pastor Chris Lamb—GIB pastor extraordinaire
Lamar Lyon—GSM American representative
Brother Lewis—associate pastor at Glen Iris Baptist Church
Lucile—visited GSM with Indiana group
Margaret—sister and friend
Mr. McKinney—my boss at Singer

Nezzie—GSM cook
Rachel—GIB member and friend
Sharon—GIB member and friend
TiFre—Haitian facial cancer patient and friend
Todo—GSM Dean of Students
Younger, Bill and Sandy—God's choice missionaries at Good Shepherd Ministry

1

Friday, February 17, 2009

We arrived in the dark of morning at the Missionary Flight International hangar. We had driven all day the previous day to arrive in plenty of time to report by 6:00 am. We were weighed together with our luggage by the staff to determine where we would sit to distribute weight evenly. The MFI DC-3 was broken, so we were driven to Fort Lauderdale for an 11:00 am departure on a tiny Lynx ten-seater.

After we were assigned seats, the pilot entered through the side window over the wing and set his Garmin GPS on the front windshield. I sat directly behind him—so close that I could count his neck hairs. There was no center aisle, and each row seated only two people almost knee to knee and wall to wall. The fellow beside me read his emergency instructions over and over, and then began reading his Bible. It looked as if he was reading in Psalm 91. The pilot pulled out his reading material: "In-flight wind conditions."

He said it is much more difficult to get a pilot's license now. When he got his, he only had to have eight hours of instruction instead of the thirty-six required now.

Did you know that when one flies from the Fort Lauderdale/ Miami International Airport to Haiti, the luggage is prematurely marked MIA? It gives one a strange unsettled feeling.

Haiti: The Lost Paradise

Our Lynx ten-passenger aircraft.

Leaving Miami
Note Garmin GPS in window

Lynda Criswell

Jack and four of our twelve passengers

This shows the full interior width of the plane.

Typical Haitian landscape

Typical Haitian landscape

Lynda exiting Lynx Air

There is a Travel Alert issued by The State Department of The United States warning U S citizens to exercise a high degree of caution when traveling to Haiti. I was told that a Travel Alert means that the government does not have to rescue you if there is a problem. Fortunately, I was also told that Missionary Flights International would get you out if they brought you in. Thank you, God.

There was a brief layover in the Bahamas for fuel. As we flew over the tropical waters, I could see numerous small islands surrounded by irregular rings of white sand, which were then surrounded by concentric rhythmic swirls of aqua and teal water. There were large compounds of luxury houses, all with privacy fences and the kind of yachts seen in luxury magazines.

The pilot pointed out Cuba as we flew low over it. Another passenger warned that you weren't supposed to fly over Cuba, but there it was.

There was the Haiti Cap Haitien International (yes, international) Airport. *Are they sure?* I wondered. The runway was cracked and weeds were growing in it. The sidewalk to the small, not quite square main building was submerged in mud in low spots. Leaning shacks and tall weeds surrounded the property. People were lounging around outside.

This really is the Cap Haitien
International Airport.

Air traffic control in Cap Haitien

Haiti: The Lost Paradise

United Nations building, Cap Haitien

United Nations in Cap Haitien

It was around 3:00 PM. Bill and Sandy Younger, the missionaries at Good Shepherd Ministry, were waiting for us. Aimee, a thirteen-year-old girl who was left at the mission gates eleven years ago, was with them.

As soon as we walked out of the terminal, people aggressively began trying to grab our bags, but we had been warned not to let them, since they would demand money if they even picked something up.

We left customs and walked through crushes of beggars and stagnant puddles of garbage water to reach the jeep Bill borrowed from Christian, the GSM overseer. Like good Americans, we snapped on our seat belts for the trip to the mission. Sandy said we must be the only people in Haiti to put on seat belts. We soon found out why.

The city was a confusion of garbage, standing putrid water, traffic going every direction, assorted loud car horns, people on foot and on heavily loaded bicycles and motorbikes threading closely through traffic, and continuous tiny leaning shops selling miscellaneous junk. I saw no new merchandise or American-style stores. Intersections did not have rights-of-way or traffic lights, so traffic nosed bumper to bumper through them at all angles, often resulting in a standstill snarl of assorted vehicles. Street lanes were not marked, so traffic could come at you the full width of the street. Bicycles and motorcycles carrying multiple passengers and wide loads wove in and out of traffic, close enough to be touched from our jeep. There were no cross walks for pedestrians, so they crossed anywhere. Carcasses of vehicles abandoned beside the street had piles of trash and broken glass under them, indicating that they had been there for some time. Several of the buildings had huge holes in their roofs; some were covered with a tarp and some weren't. Some appear to have collapsed long ago and been abandoned. There are no construction codes here so reinforced concrete has little meaning. There does not appear to be any effort to clean up the debris, possibly due to lack of equipment and/or funds.

Many of the houses looked as if they had been under construction for some time. Bill said some Haitians worked in America and sent money back to Haiti to build for themselves a nice retirement home.

Women with perfect posture balanced impossible loads in large, creative containers on their heads. They turned, bent over, and stooped, but never dropped their burdens. Some had cloth pads under their head containers. Perhaps that created a more comfortable stable shelf on a rounded head.

Downtown Cap Haitien

Haiti: The Lost Paradise

Normal City Traffic.
No dividing lines on the road.

Street vendors displaying merchandise

The ten miles of federal road from Cap Haitien to Milot took over an hour to drive because Bill had to drive slowly to negotiate the continuous deep pits and ruts in the road. The first time the car seat dropped away from me and the seat belt cut into my body was a shock. Within a few minutes my lower back became sore from the rub-board-like action. The seat belt came off.

The scenery was captivating. There were small stick-and-stucco huts, primitive and art-worthy bridges over drainage ditches, thick dust over everything, women walking with their various containers on their heads, and thin, dispirited horses, cows, goats, roosters, chickens, and dogs with lowered heads.

Bridge over drainage ditch

Bridge over drainage ditch

Cart in Milot

The people generally do not feed their animals, so one does not see the prancing horses and frisky dogs we see in America. Their animals also do not receive medical attention, so it is common to see a heavily burdened donkey or horse with untreated open wounds. This seems shortsighted to Americans.

People were washing clothes, motorbikes, and children in the muddy creeks that meandered by the road. Aging garbage was strewn everywhere since the Haiti government does not supply any garbage pickup service. Occasionally a scrap of paper wheeled by in the dust. My head swiveled to take it all in.

People and animals here defecate on the ground. The heat dries it, and winds blow it. People walking breathe it. This can cause worms to develop in people's stomachs and come out of their mouths due to the lack of sanitary precautions.

If a dead person is discovered in public, the people will not touch the corpse unless it is a relative because they could be held responsible for the death, for which the penalty is death.

If a vehicle breaks down, the driver abandons it. Eventually the people steal parts from it until nothing is left. Bill once saw a large road grader, including the huge blade, gradually disappear over several weeks.

I am aware that we probably asked the same questions asked by numerous past visitors to Good Shepherd Mission, yet Bill and Sandy gave us fresh, friendly replies and overviews of what to expect.

We met only about four vehicles on the hour journey to Milot, but as we neared the mission we saw more people walking. I was excited when Bill turned into the locked gates of Good Shepherd Mission and honked the horn for the guards to let us in. As the gates swung open, I saw my home for the next few months.

There were several buildings, all surrounded by a ten-foot-tall concrete block fence and interrupted by several locked gates. It was carefully maintained, but not excessive or showy. Bill parked the jeep beside the main building, and he and Sandy left us alone in our apartment to get settled.

Our apartment was small and well planned. The living room, bedroom, bathroom, and kitchen fanned out from the entry foyer. Through the locked iron gates over the side door in the living room, I could see the vocational school and high school where Jack and I would be working. We were told to close and lock that door before dark or roaches would come in through the open spaces at the bottom. We followed those instructions.

Mardi Gras started Monday, but the first parade went by the front gates the afternoon we arrived. We were told that normal people stayed inside. Their music was discordant and strident. The women were dancing and moving suggestively. The marchers were unorganized and appeared angry. The costumes were frightful. Several men were covered with dead banana leaves from head to foot, with only their dark eyes uncovered. They were snapping long whips over the people. One of the men cracked a whip just beside my head toward the concrete drainage wall in front of the mission, and a huge chunk of concrete broke off. Shocked and indignant, I looked up and met his eyes. My stomach constricted and I felt as if I would throw up. I was stunned by the emptiness and evil I saw in his angry eyes.

I felt it was prudent that I return to the safety of the mission.

Sandy explained to me that they were *RahRah*—Satan worshippers.

RahRah Parade

Mardi Gras spook

Lynda Criswell

Excitement was running high for classes to begin next week. My classroom will be a showplace, thanks to the generosity of Glen Iris Baptist Church members and friends.

Ladies of Glen Iris, the patterns you copied are treasures! From your generous hands to a plastic storage container to a storage area in a mission at Milot, God has provided.

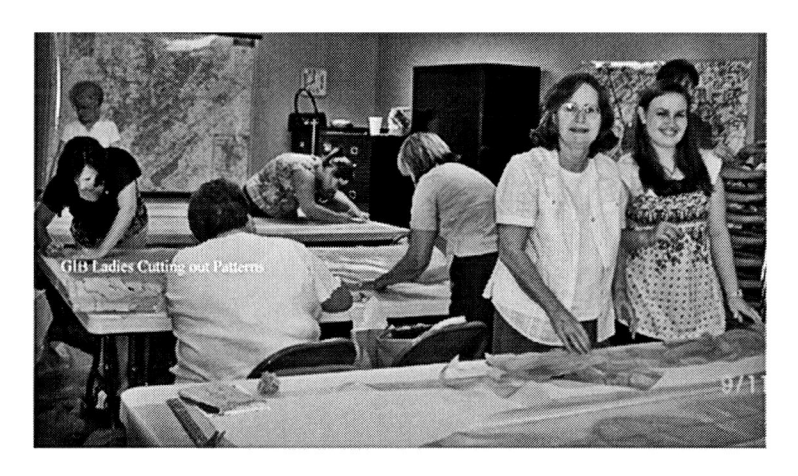

Ladies cutting out patterns

Anticipating class

I was told to guard all of the supplies, even if they are of no value. I took all the machine accessories out of the machines and will check them out individually to the students.

One of the guard dogs appears to love me. They call him Bear (appropriately), but I think his real name is NoBear, because that is what most people call him. They also have Cali, a calico cat, and Luki, Bear's mother.

The house of BeBe, one of the guards here, caught on fire last night. He lost everything except his mattress, but his family is safe. He had two rooms.

Thanks to my wonderful family who are taking care of my house, cats, mail, and bills. I love each of you.

Lynda,
So Blessed

2

Wednesday, February 18, 2009

Roosters awakened us at 5:57 AM. Sandy fixed our breakfast of pancakes grapefruit, and bananas after morning devotions. Everyone working or living on the GSM campus meets in an upstairs room across from the main house. Each morning at 6:30 AM they study a chapter as they work their way through the Bible. Visitors are welcome and often come. Bill answers questions for them. Most of these people have had no access to a Bible, much less a commentary, so Bill's insight into the scriptures is a treasure.

We began moving our supplies to our classrooms. The scissors and rulers that were donated, my sunhat, an iron, a sewing machine, and other items were missing. We were told that items often disappear in customs.

Lunch was peanut butter and jelly sandwiches, potato chips, and Little Debbie cakes.

We drove back to Cap Haitien for supplies, again borrowing Christian's jeep. Bill and Sandy treated us to dinner at a restaurant that used to be the palace of King Christophe's queen. It was elegant, beautifully landscaped, and spacious. Vendors selling their souvenirs sat under the huge entrance trees. The restaurant was empty at 5:00 PM except for us. The menu offered beef, chicken, or goat. The animal was killed when the meal was ordered. I chose pepper steak, fried bananas, French fries, beans and rice and carrots, and *colcum*. This is a whitish vegetable with the texture of cooked carrots. It was often on the menu at the mission.

Haiti: The Lost Paradise

Entrance to former palace of Queen
Now a restaurant

Lynda, Sandy, Aimee, Bill and Jack inside restaurant

Bill sometimes has to go to a money exchanger in Cap Haitien. He enters a private room where they have guns and security cameras. Only he is allowed in. They guard him until he is back in the car.

We went to the French bakery to get the week's supply of bread. The display cases were full of tempting, well displayed items. This bakery seemed out of place amid the litter just outside its door.

Begging children approached the car continually. Bill had to drive away slowly because they would not move away.

Last night I had my first cold shower. When it is rainy or cloudy, the solar panels do not get enough sun to warm the water for us. Tonight promises another cold shower.

Bedtime tonight is 7:00 PM.

Lynda,
The mouth of Haiti

3

Thursday, February 19, 2009

Sandy fixed scrambled eggs and biscuits and guava jelly for breakfast The eggs are straight from the chickens with no additives, so the white will not firm up for fried eggs.

I spent the morning setting up and organizing my classroom. God has literally supplied all of our needs.

My classroom can be seen easily from the high school, so there were a lot of visitors. Students, parents, employees, and teachers are naturally curious about all the activity and new items being brought into the room. Several of the high school-aged young men asked me to tutor them in English. They know that being able to speak English is a great asset. I explained that I was sorry, but I would not have time.

Lunch was tuna sandwiches, bananas, and chips. Dinner was baked spaghetti, salad, and fried bananas. I am embarrassed at how much I ate.

Tonight we had warm showers because there was enough sun for the solar heaters to heat the water.

Lynda,
Learning

4

Friday, February 20, 2009

Breakfast was oatmeal and raisins after the morning devotions.

I am still working on my classroom. I also met with my interpreter, FiFi, and Nola, the teacher I am going to train.

Lunch was peanut butter and jelly sandwiches. I updated e-mail addresses for Jack most of the afternoon.

Dinner was rice, bean sauce, coleslaw, and bananas.

God has reminded me of the commissioning service Glen Iris held for us on February 15. I looked over the dear congregation that night and felt such a God-given love for them. Jack and I sat on the front row, and each staff member walked behind us, praying for us individually, touching our shoulders. Mr. Adams prayed that it was an honor for him to pray for us, and I was humbled. I was overwhelmed with God's love and guidance in my life.

Ralph, one of McDonald's ROMEOs (Retired Old Men Eating Out), honored us by attending the service. He gave me a journal to record my experiences.

All of my family members were there except for one. My son Jack was grinning, along with his wife, Cynthia, and his children, Cara and Schaeffer. I cried on Wes's shoulder and saw his wife, Kristy, shedding happy tears. We lingered late. My grandson Wesley and his fiancée, Kristy, were there. God covered me with a sense of fulfillment and joy.

I felt that perhaps the reason for my life in Christ was ahead.

Lynda,
Blessed

5

Saturday, February 21, 2009

Breakfast was French toast. Bill and Jack worked on sanding and painting the doors to the classrooms.

Sandy introduced me to the washing machine just down the hall. She explained that the detergent must be dissolved by swishing it in the water before the clothes are added because it does not automatically dissolve. There is only cold water for the washer, which is not a problem.

Clothes are solar dried. We hang them outside. I love doing that.

Sandy is outside fixing Aimee's hair in the sunshine, using the professional supplies sent by Sophia from GIB. Thank you, Sophia, for having a heart for a child you did not know.

In Haiti one out of every eight children die before the age of five.

Pray that I will have the gift of language.

Lynda,
Learning

6

Sunday, February 22, 2009

We awoke at 6:00 AM to beautiful a cappella singing coming from the church on the GSM property. I call it TheChurchontheProperty, as it did not seem to have another name.

After morning devotions and a grapefruit and cereal breakfast, we drove a short distance from Milot to attend a church there that was pastored by a Good Shepherd Ministry graduate. We sat on the first row on narrow wooden benches like everyone else. Someone brought one of the two electric fans and turned it directly on us, the spoiled Americans. The other was directed at their pastor. This was humbling.

Church close to Milot

The church service was quite interesting. They sang for an hour and had preaching for an hour. Several people slept. There was a small electric piano. We were told that the pianists usually do not know the songs ahead of time. They listen to the singers and play random chords until they figure it out.

Most of the singing there was also a cappella and perfect. A women's ensemble stood in a tight semi-circle right beside us and sang several songs. The congregation wore their best clothes, although the clothes were worn and old by American standards. Women do not wear sleeveless tops. Children are dressed in finery as if it were Easter.

I do not know much about the lizard that repeatedly climbed the wall behind the pastor and fell off into the choir.

A dog stood at the entrance, then moved to the front row where we were seated. He was so skinny that I thought at first that he was a goat. When he stretched, his middle was about eight inches in circumference. No one else seemed to notice him. He eventually wandered out.

The church recognized us as visitors. We probably looked like two light bulbs in the Haitian congregation.

As Bill drove down the road, children called to us to give them "dolla." We had been told not to. The children call Jack *blanc scheesh*, or cheap white man. Bill says I am *bla*n*cette*. We were also warned that the people often resent having their picture taken. That is understandable. No one would want to feel like an oddity. They often expect you to pay them if they allow you to take a picture.

Lunch was egg salad sandwiches.

Bill walked us down the road to meet BeBe's family and see what the fire last week did to his house. His tin roof was scorched, and his belongings and clothes burned. The grill that indicated his kitchen area was located outside, so that area was not harmed.

Most of the families live in a group of huts together, with stick fences providing a loose separation. This is also how BeBe's family lived. Jack took a video camera loaned to us by Ken at our church. The children were fascinated at seeing themselves on video. He also had to take still pictures of all of them repeatedly.

BeBe and Bill approaching the back entrance to BeBe's house

BeBe's house and mattress after the fire

BeBe's kitchen

We ate baked spaghetti, coleslaw, and cake for supper. Sandy and I went up to the classroom to play with fabric afterwards.

Dorothy, a missionary from Port-au-Prince, is staying here to take her friend TiFre to the hospital just down the street in Milot for surgery tomorrow with an American medical team. TiFre had cancer in his jaw, so they removed his jaw last year and replaced it with metal. Tomorrow they will graft part of his hip bone to his jaw. He will need another surgery next year.

The hospital does not supply medicine, food, or baths. Dorothy is paying for his surgery. He can stay there a week, but Dorothy has to feed him pureed food which she has to provide, bathe him, give him his medicine, and do anything else that is done for him. Then they will drive a full day back to Port-au-Prince over the rutted road, hoping they do not hurt his stitches.

I asked how she met him. She said he came with her yard.

Dorothy intended to sleep in her truck during the week of TiFre's care. She asked Bill if she could park inside our locked gates. He invited her to stay in the dormitory and eat with us instead.

When there is company, the mission has a cook, Nezzie, and a helper, Inno. The food is plentiful and simple. Fried plantains, beans and rice, and coleslaw are often on the menu. I noticed large worms working in the cabbage thrown in the garbage can. Dorothy said that was common. You just learn to deal with it; they get most of them out.

The people here are impressed with the new *leskol* (school) for *koud* (sewing). GSM students and teachers constantly wander over to look through the bars and the classroom door as I am working to set up the room. None of the doors or windows have glass, but they all have bars and screens. I had to lock the door at times because of the interruptions from the curious onlookers. I wore the door key on a red ribbon on my left wrist.

There was no need for a purse here, so mine stayed forgotten in our apartment.

I am so thrilled that you gave at God's command. He has blessed this ministry richly.

My upper-floor classroom door and front windows face the high school across the courtyard. As I worked in my room, I often saw students kneeling just outside their classroom door on the concrete sidewalk. Bill said the teachers seem to prefer this method of discipline. He isn't sure what it accomplishes except sore knees.

BeBe, Bill, Lynda, Christian, Joselyn, and ToTo
Setting up the classroom

The people here have not seen embroidery machines, and stare at the wall hangings I made—especially the complicated dense embroideries showing the Singer Featherweight machine. I have told them that my machine embroidered them, but they do not seem to believe that.

I translated several pertinent Bible verses using an Internet English-to-Creole program to machine embroider my wall decorations in advance. These translations are not always accurate. I have asked some of the Haitian visitors who parade through my room to tell me what the verses say. I am thrilled to report that God made sure that each of them is accurate.

Pray that I will have the gift of languages.

Lynda,
The mouth of Haiti

7

Monday, February 23, 2009

Hello, from the land of promise! I am helping Sandy and Dorothy make dresses using the new methods. I taught them how to change a pattern to make it on the bias and showed them the benefits of doing so. Sandy was surprised to find she could make Aimee four skirts in an hour. They love the new methods.

This morning's devotion was read in Isaiah 30. The men come up with some unexpected questions on the text. Joscelyn, one of the employees, told about a friend of his who became a Christian and later became sick. She went to a witch doctor, returning to her old ways. After three days the witch doctor told her he could do nothing, and advised her to go to a hospital fast. She died. Joscelyn saw in Isaiah 30 the folly of returning to old ways.

Did you know that gnat bites leave a giant swollen whelp? Ask me how I know.

A Haitian selling jewelry and coconut boxes came to the gate asking for me. He said his earrings were made of the finest white gold and worth sixty American dollars. He said cruise ship people stood in line to buy from him. I offered him two American dollars. He was offended. They were worth maybe that much. They looked like aluminum. He offered me two pairs for sixty American dollars. I offered him two dollars again. We finally agreed on five American dollars for two pairs. I did not buy any of his coconut boxes.

I was told later that he bragged about how much I had paid him.

The per capita 2008 income in Haiti was $1,300.

An employee here has worked for the cruise ships. He told me that they set up an artificial tropical scene on the shore for the tourists. They hire the vendors and supply what they sell and set the prices.

Bill and Christian are still negotiating with the Haitian woman I am supposed to train to take over the sewing class. She seems experienced in basic hand sewing.

People here do not understand why the Youngers feed their two dogs and one cat. They feel animals are to be used, not fed. The Youngers have explained that the animals work for them just as their employees do and deserve food and support. And Bear can keep people away from the gate.

Bill told me about driving at night in poor visibility and turning a corner just as two people on a motorcycle came speeding around him from the other direction. When they got beside his truck, they hit a pit and went flying in the air. He took them to a hospital and waited in the waiting room. Soon the room filled with people. They were all saying that Bill hit the two people.

Do you know what the penalty is for that? If a person hits someone with his car and the injured person dies, they put him in his car and set it on fire.

He kept saying he did not hit them, but someone said they saw it happen. He was getting a little uneasy when a very young girl came forward and said she saw the whole thing, and Bill did not hit them. He wondered if she was an angel sent by God.

The crowd let him walk untouched through them.

A lady here with facial cancer had been going to witch doctors until she ran out of money to pay them. Her husband came to Bill to see if he could help. He took pictures of her face to send to the American doctors. She has a newborn baby and other children.

I am working on translations of sewing machine parts today and we are taking classes on language at night. Dorothy just happens to have written a book on the Haitian Creole language.

I told you I was asking for the gift of language. God sent me a teacher exactly one week before classes began who wrote the Haitian language book. Imagine that! What a God!

Imagine living between two witch doctors. Joscelyn does.

Lynda,
Thankful

8

Wednesday, February 25, 2009

$\mathcal{D}$orothy is also writing a book on Haitian tourist attractions. She asked Sandy and me to go with her to see where cocoa in Haiti originates.

Milot is about a five-minute walk west of Good Shepherd Ministry's front gate. It is the third largest city in Haiti. The hospital here is where TiFre had his operation with the American medical team. There are three main streets. Most of the streets do not have sidewalks. The paving is broken and uneven. There is the ubiquitous, strangely elaborate, paved drainage ditch wandering unevenly down one side that theoretically takes garbage away when it rains. Litter is omnipresent and garbage pickup is nonexistent anywhere in Haiti. An occasional house will show an attempt at beautification with wild hibiscus plants or other greenery. The streets are dusty. Windows have bars and screens. People sit outside their doors on faded plastic chairs or narrow weathered wooden benches to avoid the heat inside. Laundry is spread on dusty cactus hedges to dry.

Main street Milot

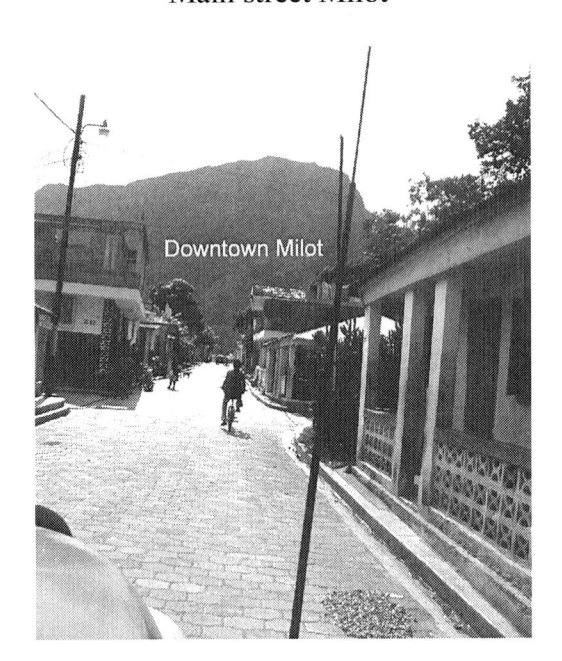

Downtown Milot

Cacao trees are abundant here. The mission has many. A child at the mission school showed me how to suck out the creamy white coating just under the shell to savor the vanilla flavor surrounding the actual cacoa bean. He told me he used to go to school here, but his father died and now his family cannot afford school for him.

The inside of a cacoa bean

Dorothy parked her truck at the house where the woman makes the cocoa, effectively blocking the narrow street for other vehicle traffic. This was not a problem because there was no other vehicle traffic. The house-shop was about eight feet wide, and the door was about three feet from the street.

The house were cocoa begins

All the houses are adjacent, but not necessarily in a straight line. They are made of sticks coated with dirt, stucco, or wood scraps. A very few have concrete walls. Most of them lean. I doubt there was a ninety-degree wall in sight. The roofs are usually rusty tin, but a few are concrete. Some have weathered wooden doors. Others have faded cloth strung over the door opening.

Quickly a crowd gathered to watch the *blancs* watch the cocoa process. Children nude from the waist down stared at us in wonder from their mother's laps. Curious teens circled to study us better. Foot traffic in the street picked up noticeably. Two roosters scooted past in a hurry.

There was a dog in the street that was so thin he seemed unable to move. He just stood with his head and tail down, his eyes sad. His fur was gone in most areas. He had two fur tufts on his hips. His eyes were haunting. One could see every bone in his body. If I could have fed him, it would have only prolonged his agony.

Dorothy documenting the making of cocoa

Lynda Criswell

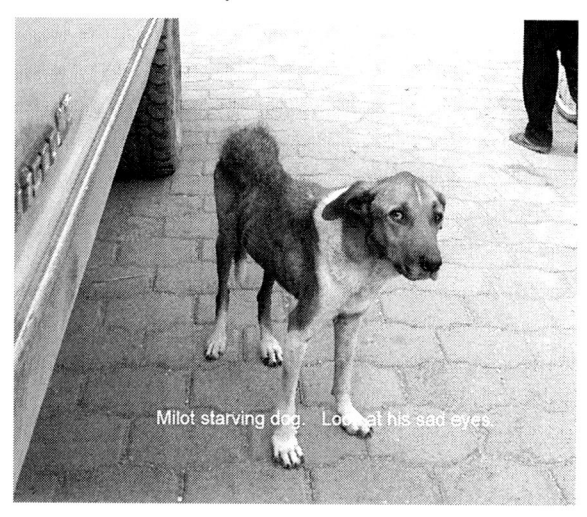

Milot starving dog. Look at his sad eyes.

Starving dog

It is common to see dogs with their noses to the ground seriously searching for any scrap of food. This dog did not even have the strength to do that.

The lady made the cocoa outside. She brought out a pan full of charcoal and set it on the fire. This was topped with a large shallow woven basket full of cacao beans that had been sun dried. These beans were roasted about five minutes. Then we blancs helped her shell the hot cacao with our bare, tender, American fingers.

She shuffled the beans around in the basket, efficiently separating the beans from the shells and tossing the shells out of the basket onto the street in one smooth operation.

This lady is a supplier of cocoa to the chocolate manufacturers of the world. She and her husband ship 150 pounds of cocoa at a time to the manufacturer.

Then we walked parade style through Milot to the grinder. People peered around corners to watch our procession.

We had to walk past the mayor's house to get there. It was easy to know which house was his as he had used dark rocks and paint to spell out "Mairie de Milot" repeatedly in the white stucco. I wondered if his job is a lifetime position.

We walked past the tailor's shop. He had his machine in a warped wooden cabinet chained to a tree in front of his house as there was not room for it inside his two-room house.

House of the Mayor of Milot

Milot's tailor

The grinder was actually about eight blocks away, located at the end of a tiny, narrow, crooked dirt path behind several houses. I had pictured a small cocoa factory with grinding machinery, stainless steel equipment, and employees.

It was only a household metal grinder mounted waist high to a sawed-off tree in a dirt backyard. Most of us have seen or owned one of these grinders. Orange peels were draped nearby in tree limbs to dry. They sell the peels to perfume makers.

Grinding factory in operation. Note orange peels hung in trees to dry.

Milot's grinding factory

The grinder was oozing with aging cocoa, but our beans were ground in it and the thick liquid was poured into four tiny rusty metal pans of perhaps two inches by four inches to cool overnight. We can pick them up in the morning. They cost $1.50 each, plus fifty cents for using the grinder. This extra fifty cents was obviously an afterthought that they figured we blancs could pay.

Dorothy made notes and took pictures to illustrate her book. I may be in her book shelling cacao beans.

We also visited a sandwich shop in Milot. The owner was a friend of Dorothy's. The man had one employee in a shop about ten feet wide and fifteen feet long. There was a worn wooden countertop that did double duty as a table, possibly large enough to seat two small people who wanted to sit close together. There were empty display cases and handwritten price lists on the wall. The only actual food I saw was one prepackaged peanut butter and cracker item.

Many of the people sell whatever they can in front of their houses.

Would you like shoes, clothes, or an iron?

The nightly language classes with Dorothy are intense. Her book is a treasure. Although French is required in the schools, most of the people do not like it and prefer Haitian, but there is no unified Haitian language. Her book can provide that language unity from her years of experience living here and studying their language.

Language study
Lynda, Dorothy, Aimee, Sandy, and Bill

Dorothy recently made a short trip away from her home in Port-au-Prince and returned to find that a child had gotten sick and the witch doctors had taken her. She went to them and demanded the girl back. They began to issue curses and would not give her the girl. She told them, "My God is stronger than your god, so give her to me!" She took the girl and ran out with the witch doctors cursing. She said she kept praying, "God, send me lots of angels right now!" All the Haitians at our morning devotions agreed with her about the power of Satan.

Ransom is never paid to kidnappers. The victim will be killed or tortured regardless.

We have set up the dining room as a sewing area. Dorothy, Sandy, and I are sewing constantly. They have each made beautifully fitted bias dresses. I hope my students are this excited to sew.

The start of classes is still indefinite. The Haitian teacher has not committed yet.

The high school teacher saw our new sewing machines and was envious. He told me that I should not use them until he tries them this fall. These machines are better than anything here.

Thanks to all of you who donated.

Lynda,
Blessed

9

Thursday, February 26, 2009

Dorothy stopped to visit a mechanic friend several months ago. When she came back to her truck that she had parked and locked, the starter had been taken out and was torn apart into each separate piece. Two men were standing there and told her that her starter was broken. She said it was not broken when she last started it. Her friend agreed that they were using her. He thought they may have broken a wire so the truck would not start. The men agreed to fix the wire for her but had to go get a part. It took them two hours to return. They billed her six hundred dollars. After some arguing, she offered them one hundred and fifty dollars. One of the men called her a name and threw the money back at her. She took the money and left.

Be thankful for America and real police.

After morning devotions and a pancake breakfast, we went to visit TiFre in the hospital. The front entrance was a strange spot for a social area. Vendors set up on the front lawn area to sell grilled mystery meat, vegetables, and food items unknown to me. Multiple clotheslines displayed used clothing from America and other items for sale. Children play. The ground is wet from last night's rain. The sick and visitors lounge around in the shade at the front entrance under a large tree. Everyone watches the blancs.

Entrance to intensive care

Hospital courtyard with chickens

Roosters and chickens wander aimlessly through the open doors and in the courtyard and into the rooms. We went around to the side entrance for intensive care and after-surgery care. I could see about four patients, and they all had advanced facial cancers. The American doctor seemed tired and overworked, but glad to meet us and give us an update on TiFre.

My heart went out to this doctor and others like him. They all come on their own funds and their own time and bring their own medical supplies.

We went to the recovery room to see TiFre. He was obviously in much pain and swollen greatly but tried to smile at us. The nurses had not been giving him the medicine Dorothy had left for him. Dorothy explained to TiFre he would have to take it himself. He tried to force a smile and look brave, but his pain was so severe he could hardly move.

The surgery patient on the bed slightly behind us was also in pain. He tried to grab my clothes to beg us for water. Dorothy asked at the nurses' station, but they said they had nothing. His rusty IV was empty of fluids.

As we left the hospital, we detoured by the infant intensive care unit. There were about ten isolation units with tiny babies separate from the other newborns. There were no nurses attending to them. Most of them were totally silent and unmoving. One was screaming and shaking convulsively. This was the only place I saw that had no screens on the windows.

I had to leave.

Lynda,
Humbled

10

Friday, February 27, 2009

    After devotions and an oatmeal breakfast, we women settled in for a day of sewing. I made two skirts each for Nessie and Inno, five skirts for Aimee, four skirts for the women in BeBe's family who lost all their clothes in the fire, and three pair of pants for TiFre, who only owned two worn pair and they were too large for him. I helped Sandy and Dorothy use the new methods to make four dresses. I was in my element and loving every minute.

Inno, Dorothy, Lynda, and Sandy sewing

    This afternoon was spent typing computer lessons for Jack's classes and putting final touches on my classroom. Bill and Jack did maintenance on some window screens. Dinner was beans and rice, carrots, and salad, with cinnamon raisin rolls for dessert.

Jack and Bill fixing screens

Quiet classroom before classes begin

Lynda Criswell

Sewing room from entry door

Left side of classroom seen from entry door

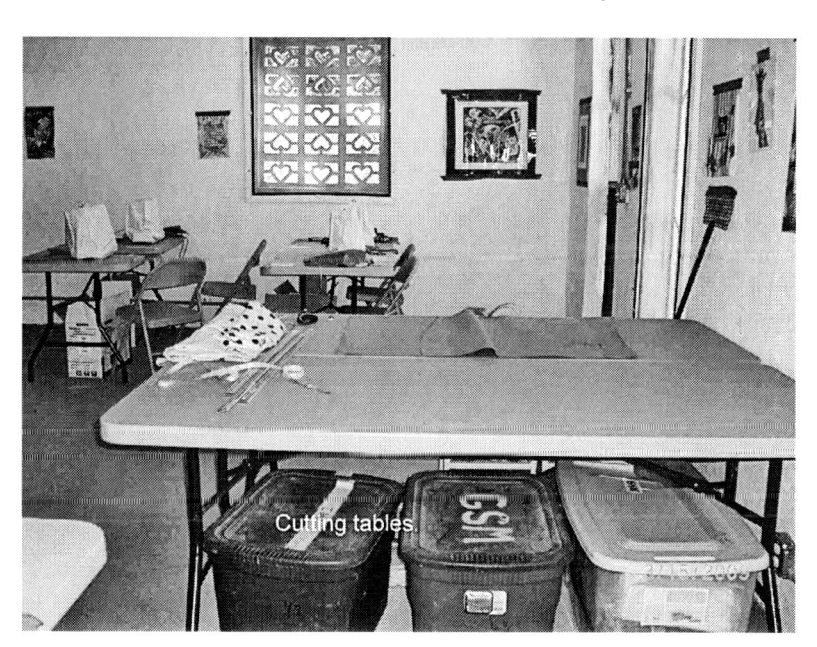

Cutting tables

Cutting tables

Jack's computer class will be made up of the following students:

Christian, GSM superintendent
Gourneau, administrator of all GSM schools
Guy, GSM grammar school principal
Hilaire, GSM French teacher
James, GSM school secretary
Johny, GSM Biology teacher
Toto, GSM dean of students

Training these employees first will boost the efficiency of GSM.

Computer class ready to set up

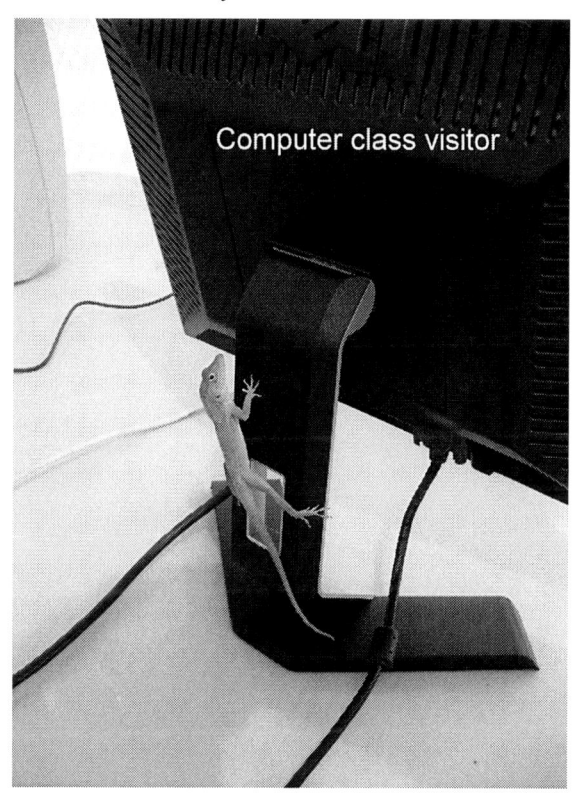

Computer class mascot

    Dorothy and TiFre will be leaving tomorrow. I went to his room to say good-bye. With great effort and pain, he stood on his healing hip bones and gave me a big smile and a hug. He was wearing a pair of his new pants.
    I cried. I will miss them both.

Lynda,
Eternity—Smoking or Nonsmoking?

11

Monday, March 2, 2009

*F*irst sewing class is today!

God has given us a fantastic day here in Haiti! There was heavy rain until about 1:30 PM, when it cleared for class at 2:00. Only one student was there by 2:15 PM. By 2:30, seven young women were there. Bill had warned me that they might not show up until very late. It seems that is the Haitian way.

Class is over at 4:00 PM because Bill has to turn off the generator then.

I told them that the first one there each day would get a sticker, with a prize each week for the most stickers. I have made a sack to hold all the donated jewelry that we will use for rewards. All the girls said they would be first tomorrow. Enthusiasm was running high.

The devotion from Proverbs 31 was about how often fabric shows up in the life of the Proverbs woman and how it is good quality fabric. Each day this week I plan to expand on Proverbs 31. The girls crowd extremely close to me when we have devotions or prayer. They seem to be hanging on my every word—or my interpreter FiFi's every word. Many times she has had to look up my words in her Creole to English dictionary. Perhaps my Southern vocabulary combined with my accent is causing her problems.

Is "y'all" a word?

Is "y'all all" a word?

Today the girls learned about fabric quality and chose fabrics for valises (tote bags) with mash (straps). FiFi was in line for fabric. She said she wanted to take this class, too. I felt honored.

None of them knew what silk was. I explained that it came from a worm. That did not impress them. I showed them the silk lining in the dress I was wearing. They wanted to see what else was under my dress. That did not happen.

We do a race to see who can thread her machine first. It becomes an athletic event. Each girl holds her thread at the spool as I count un, deux, trois, allez (one, two, three, go). The first one to thread to the eye of the needle raises her hand. I check to verify that it was done correctly, with no tensions or guides missed in haste. There is a sticker prize. They jump up and down and call out "Leenda!" Then they want to do it again.

Class relay excitement
Notice smiles

Classtime

We have a winner!

There are at least two extremely talented girls in this class. I will watch them and give them advanced projects.

We end class with a spirited review, reward stickers, and prayer. They all want to stay and touch me and ask me to teach them more.

I am ashamed to admit that at first I wondered if their enthusiastic attitude was only an act. They are so appreciative and excited. They are spoiling me.

A group from Indiana is staying here at the mission. They were interested in the new school. Lucile, one of the ladies, said her church group wants to adopt the sewing school, and asked what we need. Isn't it amazing how God arranged that?

We need fabric and all the things that disappeared after going through Haiti customs: yard sticks, marking pencils, scissors, and an iron.

God is so good to me. His blessings are undeserved and abundant.

What do you consider your bedtime? Here, with nothing to do at night and light only from stored power, 8:00 PM feels like a good time.

How do you like to be awakened in the morning? Here choir practice at TheChurchontheProperty does it if the roosters do not. Waking up to a cappella voices in perfect harmony singing praises should be listed on the travel brochures as an added special attraction.

However, the roosters have been silent lately.

Lynda,
God's undeserving servant in Haiti
Pray for the people

12

Tuesday, March 3, 2009

Today three students were waiting at 1:30 PM for class to begin at 2:00 PM. They got stickers. They had walked to class in the rain.

The American surgeons said they could not help the lady with advanced facial cancer. They said she probably has less than six months left.

One definition of terminal in the dictionary is a place people pass through on their way to somewhere else.

Here is another example of God's efficiency in answering prayers.

One of the sergers I brought would not work. I did troubleshooting on it but could not find the problem. I repeatedly e-mailed Mr. McKinney, my boss at the local Singer store, in a panic. If anyone could fix it across an ocean, he could. My son Wes left work to buy another serger. Mr. McKinney gave him a Haiti deal on the new one and a discount for the one that I could not get going and included several notions in the box. Mr. Lyon is going to pick it up today from Wes and have it on the plane Monday with the medical team that is headed to us.

Hard working and devoted, Mr. Lyon is also going to gather other notions for us that disappeared in customs: scissors, yardsticks, and an iron. These items are not easily available here.

Only God could have worked this out so quickly and so well. He uses His people.

It has rained all day. I made tomato sandwiches and fruit salad for dinner.

Lynda,
The mouth of Haiti

13

Wednesday, March 4, 2009

Classes were cancelled today because it had rained for twenty-four hours. How are classes cancelled when there are no telephones? You tell Christian and he gets the word around.

However, by 1:30 PM two girls had shown up hoping for class and the others were there soon, so we began class anyway. I am not hard to convince. I think I can drop the sticker reward for those who arrive first.

Christian had forty polo shirts with the GSM emblem on them that are too large for the students. They wear a different color of uniform depending on whether they are a grammar school student, a high school student, or an indentured student. I will take the shirts in for him on Saturday.

The facial cancer has eaten most of the face of the lady I mentioned earlier. She has part of one eye left. She lies in bed and cries all the time. Bill says her two-month-old baby looks sick.

After childbirth, women here pack themselves with dirty rags, which causes infections, which often leads to death due to lack of medicine. A baby without a mother or family is left on the street in front of a house in hopes someone will take it.

If an adult dies, word gets back to the family by word of mouth, and they come for the body. Until then the body is covered and left. This happens even in the hospitals.

The cemeteries have crypts above the ground with grating inside. A body is placed on the grating. When it disintegrates, they add the next dead body onto the grate.

Lynda,
Pray for the people

14

Thursday, March 5, 2009

It has rained all day and into the night. Rain means no sun, which means no solar powered hot water, which means a cold shower.

Some of you may want a better understanding of the property here.

Picture a large rectangle divided into four squares. Three of the four squares would house the school, with one of the fourths being used as the mission quarters.

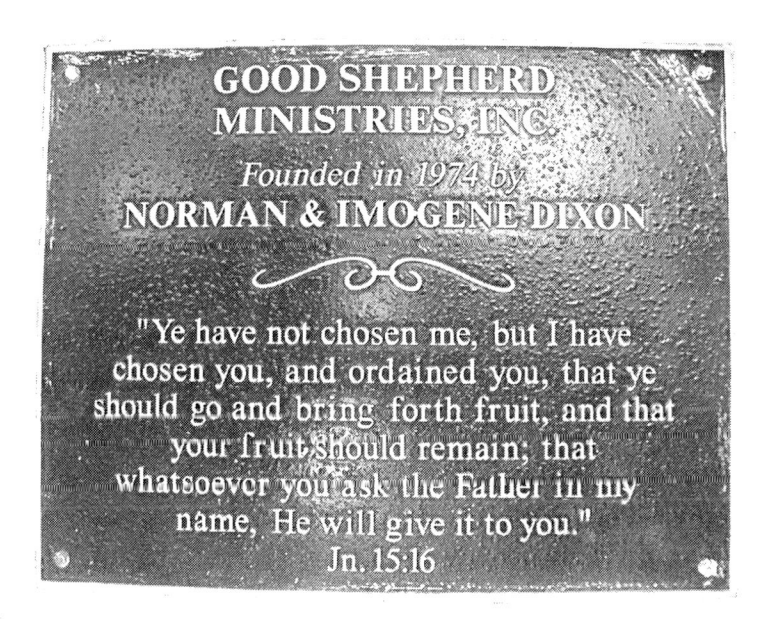

> **GOOD SHEPHERD MINISTRIES, INC.**
>
> Founded in 1974 by
> **NORMAN & IMOGENE DIXON**
>
> "Ye have not chosen me, but I have chosen you, and ordained you, that ye should go and bring forth fruit, and that your fruit should remain; that whatsoever you ask the Father in my name, He will give it to you."
> Jn. 15:16

There is a ten-foot concrete wall surrounding the complete property. The property faces north, and is on the south side of the main road from Cap Haitien to Milot. There are two locked double iron gates in the wall facing the main road in front and a small locked gate at the back southeast corner behind the vocational school. Both of the front gates are guarded twenty-four hours a day. The small back gate gives access to the hillside behind the property. Some of this hillside is planted by Good Shepherd Ministry employees for food.

Entering the property from the main road through the front west gate is the main access to the school. The first building on the east side of that gate is TheChurchontheProperty.

On the west side of that gate is the two-story concrete grammar school, then the dual-use medical and lunch room is south of that. There is a large smooth dirt area here usually busy with children. It is used as a playground and for the morning assembly. They begin singing Bible songs around 7:30 each morning.

Morning school assembly

The well is south of that. The neighborhood people come during the day to get well water as most do not have a water supply.

Children getting well water

A five-gallon bucket of water weighs forty pounds

Next is the Super Flusher. Thanks to many volunteer groups including folks from Glen Iris Baptist, there are ten roofed stalls with a toilet and a shower head in each. They can all be flushed at one time. There is also a small freestanding restroom in this area.

Super Flusher

South of the grammar school and slightly to the east is the two-story concrete high school. The vocational school is to its east and on the southeast edge of the property. It is painted a tropical pink that Bill says results when the paint store mixes together all the unsold paint colors. The store offers it free.

High School

Lynda Criswell

High School students before class

Vocational School with goat

    The two buildings face each other over a grassy courtyard area. There is a picturesque rock walkway and steps connecting them. Luxurious bright green moss and exotic ferns sprout continually in the cracks of the rocks. A landscape architect could not have done a better job. I get to walk this idyllic route several times a day.

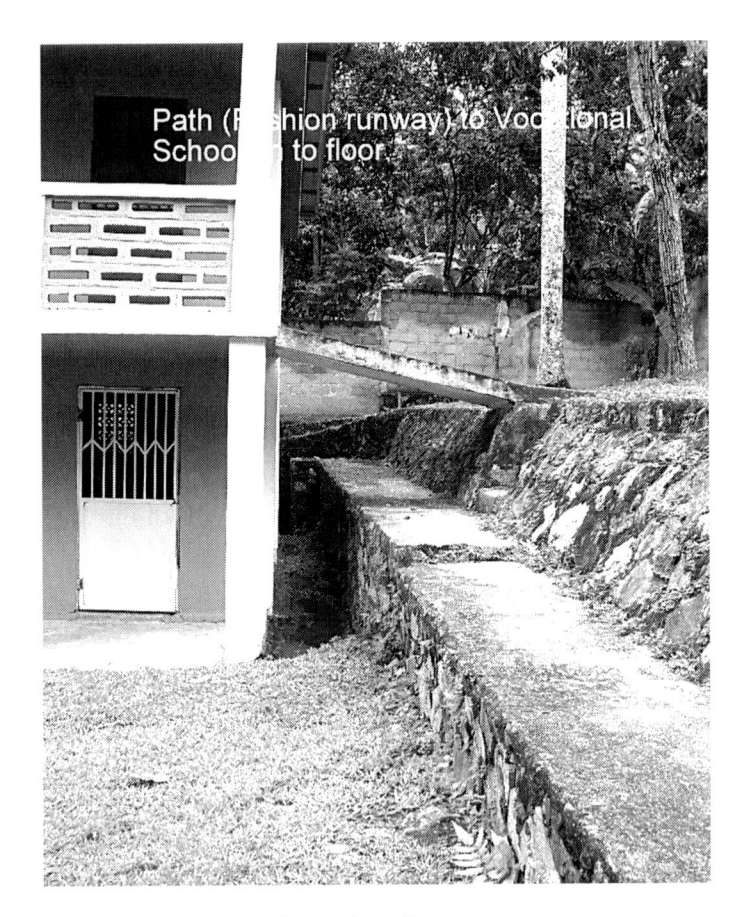

School walkway

Lynda Criswell

Steps to Sewing School

Walk to school
Future Fashion Show runway

View from school to house

In the sunny spot slightly north of these two buildings is the blue water tower with its solar panels. It creates the power to run the pump for the water for the school. Christian often has his cows or goats grazing here. Watch your step.

Entering the property from the main road through the front east gate places one in the private area of the compound. This area has its own concrete wall enclosure and sits in the upper northeast quarter.

The first building on the west inside this area is the office of the supervisor, Christian. Slightly behind his office and to the west is the depot, which contains a large tool shed and houses all the batteries that store power from the generator. The solar panel on top of this building heats water for our use.

GSM gates from inside compound

There is a grassy area between these buildings and the main house. Christian's jeep and the Good Shepherd Ministry truck park here. The Good Shepherd truck can be outfitted to haul diesel containers to be refilled, benches to transport visiting teams, or any cumbersome load.

Proudly painted on the side are the words "Mission Bon Berger" – Haitian for Good Shepherd Ministry.

The main house sits next on the west side. It is a picturesque two-story concrete house painted cream with tropical green trim. The upstairs houses the dormitories, bathrooms, kitchen, dining area, and storage. It is surrounded on three sides by a balcony. Downstairs are the Youngers' private living quarters, a laundry area, an enclosed walk, and a private three-room apartment where we live. There is a porch on three sides, covered by the upstairs balcony.

GSM main house

Our apartment entrance

West and behind this house is a separate area where the dogs can be kept.

South of the main house is a grassy area for a garden, visible from the apartment's living room side door.

Going back to the front east gate entering the private area from the main road, on the east side is a concrete two-story dark pink building. The downstairs is being made into an apartment to house visitors. The upstairs houses the air-conditioned computer room and the devotional room.

Bill trimming hibiscus hedges in front of Devotional room

View from devotional room

I can look down from this devotional room into the backyard of our neighbor, Pastor Fred, and see lush foliage through the tall breadfruit trees, children playing, and the backyard neighbor hanging her laundry on the shrubbery. Sometimes I can hear pigs rooting and squealing.

Pastor Fred's house and cybercafe adjacent the mission compound 4/4/2009

Pastor Fred's house

This east area of this private compound has a lawn, hibiscus hedges, and a tree with a swing. South of this area is a gate in the side of the concrete wall that leads to the garbage bin and the generator house. This wall also has a locked double gate in the middle to allow a vehicle to drive from the front east entry gate south straight through the private area, through this gate, and on to the vocational school and high school on the south end of the property.

This completes the private area.

This property is easily one of the best maintained I have seen here. Bill and Sandy are conscientious custodians for God.

How are all these buildings so well maintained and so many needs met when the mission is not wealthy? God puts it on the hearts of His people, who volunteer to supply time, materials, energy, or whatever is needed. Lamar Lyon coordinates the needs with those willing to fulfill them. We count it all joy.

The voodoo people and witch doctors here say they do not kill. If a child is born deformed, imperfect, or a twin, they will bury it alive. But they do not kill.

I am praying that God will prepare the hearts of each student in my class to understand and accept Jesus as her Savior. I lead devotions before and after class. I have asked God to direct these times so I can explain on their terms Who Jesus is and how God has planned for them to go to Heaven through Jesus' sacrificial death. Please pray with me.

If you have anything small you want sent to the school and can get it to Bill and Sandy's Florida address, the medical team will bring it:

We need:
non-roll elastic, one-half inch wide and three-quarters of an inch wide
metal yardsticks
marking pencils
full sized scissors

Got to go! There are ten students waiting for me at 1:15 PM although school was cancelled. Five are new students. They want a class now!
They probably want stickers.

Lynda,
The mouth of Haiti

15

Friday, March 6, 2009

Be ahead of all your friends!
Learn the newest resort trend!
Have a Haitian shower in a bucket!

You will love this back-to-basics thrill.
First, find a large bucket and a small pouring container. You will want to rinse the bucket because it probably has multiple uses. Do not think about what they are. Heat the water to boiling in a pan on top of the stove. Pour the hot water into your bucket. Run into the bathroom with the bucket, and set it on the shower floor. Standing outside the shower, turn the water on. It does not matter which faucet you use, as they both produce cold water. When the bucket has filled with cold water to dilute the boiling water, turn off the shower faucet.

Now is the time to undress and step on the cold tile shower floor to enjoy a quality primitive shower. Use a bath sponge to apply liquid soap to your body. When you are solidly soaped up, grab the small pouring container and consider where you want to aim. I start on my face, leaning back so the warm water drains down and is not wasted. I am almost proficient enough to do this without getting the water up my nose and causing me to make impolite gagging noises. Then work your way down. This may require some carefully thought-through gymnastics, but concentrate on getting the most value from the flow. After all, you are saving money by not going to your gym, right? Be stingy at redipping the sponge into the bucket.

When you become talented at this, you may find you have some warm water left. Good for you! Splurge! Redo those areas that are still a little slippery.

If you have not planned well and have run out of warm water, I hope you remembered to use moisturizing soap because some will be staying on your skin. I did tell you to use moisturizing soap, did I not?

Keep informed on the best in quality resort living in a third-world county (soon to be reclassified as a fourth-world country because they have depleted their natural resources).

Next: Hair Care in Haiti. Do not miss it!

The girls asked for a Saturday class. When I pray in class, two of the girls always say "aymeen" loudly and grin at me. I assume that means that they are in agreement.

Elvie and Luvrance finished their tote bags. Elvie centered a design on the front of hers and used coordinating fabric for trim, as any good designer would.

Jack made a video of them showing their bags and giggling because they had never seen themselves on video. Thank you again, Ken, for the use of the video camera.

I made stir fry for the Youngers and us tonight. I browned the green peppers, colcum, and onions, added the cut chicken, and simmered it all together with soy sauce. I enjoy making Southern buttermilk biscuits at home, but my effort to make them here was a failure.

Lynda,
God's undeserving blessed servant in Haiti

16

Saturday, March 07, 2009

Life Lessons
By Lynda

A constant in life I have rediscovered is the smell of wet dog.

Roosters here do not say cock-a-doodle-do. They say, "Ar-r-rrr," and pass it along to all the other roosters in their communication network. (Yes, the roosters have returned, and I am glad.)

I have figured out a reason that people here stare at me. It is not often one sees someone over thirty years old with all their teeth.

I still do not know why people in American stare at me. No suggestions, please.

Here is a novel Haitian idea for Brother Jonathan, our ten-talented Glen Iris music director. Choir practice starts here at 6:00 AM Saturday morning. It continues all day with fifteen-minute breaks between the two-hour practice sessions. He could put a sign-up list in the foyer. Perhaps he could also work in the finger snapping the men here do to keep the tempo up. This would blend well into the Glen Iris whistling tradition.

This section is not for those with tender standards of proper etiquette. Remember that there are no bathroom facilities in any of the on-site school buildings: not in the grammar school, high school, or vocational school. Homes and businesses do not usually have indoor plumbing.

See if you come to my conclusion. A student runs up to the teacher and asks that she stop teaching so the student may go to the bathroom without missing anything. Strangely, missing information was never a concern with the American students I have taught. The student is gone only a few minutes. There is a grassy area beside my room in full view of the high school.

This quick method of getting past a time-consuming need is also observed in the great twelve-square-block metropolis of Milot where there is no grassy area.

If you do find a public sink or public toilet (unfortunately, I did find one in Cap Haitien), there will be no running water and no nice homey touches like soap and toilet paper.

Thank you for sending the picture of Glen Iris in the Saturday March snow. It does look odd to see the snow, but especially it is strange to see no cars in the parking lot.

Think about what you would do if you had no generator or electricity or satellite or computer service. I am open to your suggestions. There is nothing to read here except one's Bible.

Oh.

Here is God's plan to meet all our needs without a paycheck:

*Send us to a place where there is nothing to buy.

*Let us earn our keep while we are there.

*Prove that he is sufficient for all of our needs (like the apostles Paul and John said).

*Bless us with a deep satisfaction and contentment from being in His will.

Have a good spring-forward Sunday at Glen Iris!

Lynda,
Blessed in Haiti

17

Sunday, March 08, 2009

"Mrs. Criswell,
Why are the girls being asked to pay for the class and even the materials and trims that were donated? We miss you and are praying for you daily. See you soon."

Charlotte brought up a good point in her e-mail that I haven't covered. Thanks, Charlotte. Yes, thanks to you people, the supplies were donated. However, they have found that things given freely are often not treasured or appreciated. The schools here all charge tuition, although it barely covers even the salaries. (I do not get paid.) If it were not for the generous support sent here, the mission could not operate at all.

So there will be a store open soon. I have categorized the fabric by good, better, and best, and they will be asked to purchase their fabric and notions for a minimal price per item.

Here is a good example: Last week I had a small problem in class. We do supply the fabric and notions free of charge for their first learning project: a tote bag (valise). Someone got into the supplies and was handing out expensive laces and the students were wasting it by sewing all over it before I saw and stopped them. They will be asked to pay for the lace.

Some abuse the generosity of missions by expecting everything at the mission to be free. This mission is trying to teach responsibility. They feel the future of Christianity in Haiti is in the children, and they are trying to instill Christian values in them at an early age. I know you all bought each item and carefully, willingly, generously felt led of God to donate it. I will be a good steward for you and God.

America built and financed a power plant here. The monthly charge for electricity is modest. Unfortunately, so many have illegally tapped into the power lines that there is no power available a short distance from the plant.

Many people here and in America find a way to purchase expensive cell phone minutes regularly, but want others to supply their needs.

Perhaps you have noticed that some on welfare in America only want more. Perhaps we could learn from the missions here. Good things do not come without a price. The best things demand a high price. Our salvation demanded the highest price.

Charlotte, thanks for giving me the opportunity to expound on this ... probably much more than you wanted!

We watched GIB's Sunday School of the Air today on an ten-inch computer screen in the second-floor dining room with a surprisingly chilly tropical breeze blowing over us. Brother Lewis was accompanied by live Haitian music from TheChurchontheProperty You could hear the witch doctors' drums coming from the other direction. It was somber symbolism.

Thank you all for allowing us the privilege and multiple blessings of representing you here. So many of you have given items, money, time, and prayer in response to God's leading. My family is busy adding my mail, bills, household chores, cat tending, and errands to their own. I deeply appreciate their sacrifice and loving support. You are a treasured people.

This is Sunday. Here are some physical things God has given me for which I am thankful:

Jesus
My family
My personal Bible
The people of Glen Iris Baptist Church
America
My life
My books
Doctors
The Sewing Expo

The spiritual blessings are innumerable, and God is multiplying them. Pray for tomorrow's classes. So much is at stake; so many are lost.

Yesterday we went to Cap Haitien again. As we left Milot, I was looking out the window when a family flipped their goat over and cut its belly open. The cry it gave was indescribable. They began immediately to gut it alive. When we came back seven hours later, they were selling roasted goat.

The drainage ditches that run beside the road are where people dump their garbage. Theoretically, when it rains, the rain washes the garbage away. It does not happen that way. They also wash their clothes and motorcycles in the same ditch when there is water in it.

Just so you know, Good Shepherd Ministries does not dump garbage on the street. We have a concrete enclosure about six feet high and fifteen feet square on the property where garbage is dumped and regularly burned. It was described earlier. They learned to puncture holes in aerosol cans before burning them. You probably know why. You're welcome.

Garbage pit duty
Ronnie, Lamar and BeBe

We were told that the people in Haiti have killed all the snakes because they hate them. However, yesterday the employees here found a snake skin about two and a half feet long by the garbage pit. They brought it, hanging on a stick, to Sandy. She did not want it.

We went to the open market. Think farmer's market, except that every aisle is dirt with a trough down the middle full of water or mud and garbage. Aisles are about five feet wide, but there are two rows of people walking in them. I learned to walk on the edges of the path to avoid most of the unctuous oily slime puddled in the center of the path.

At intersections, the standing water is often too wide to jump, so we all scuttle around the sides and hope we do not get that rich water on us. The intersections are also where the garbage accumulates forever.

Anyone want to walk here?

The path where you have to walk

Dorothy said Port-au-Prince built drainage ditches twenty feet wide before she went to America on furlough. When she returned in a month, the ditches were completely full of garbage. Of course, we know that eternally standing garbage produces side effects on our health besides the stench.

This is not the bad section of town. This is town at its best.

Sandy had many items to buy, so we rented a wheelbarrow. This transaction includes a man who maneuvers the wheelbarrow and your purchases and delivers them to your vehicle.

The major part of the market is roofed. Under the roof there are numerous large nests with whitewash coatings from birds or other animals.

Fresh colorful vegetables are artistically arranged in pyramids and designs in many vendor stalls. Some of the vegetables are ones I do not recognize. The smell of mystery meat roasting over mahogany charcoal permeates the area. I see a skinny cat watching hopefully. A child is urinating. Another child is staring at us from behind her Mother with a combination of curiosity and fear. Someone is singing. A loud animated argument breaks out close by. I move closer to Bill.

Vegetable display

See anything you need?

Haiti: The Lost Paradise

Vendor

Lynda shopping

Am I in line?

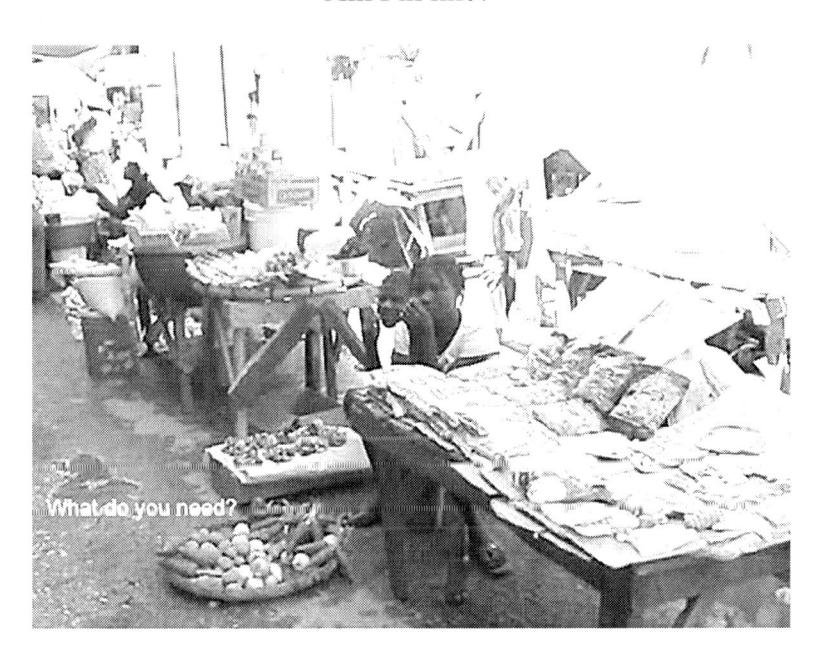

What do you need?

Sandy negotiated prices at several vendors she knows. Dry goods are scooped out of large open sacks into smaller sacks for us. The wheelbarrow was full.

We went to the sections of *twals* (fabrics). Fabric was stacked six feet high on leaning wooden shelves in booths about six feet wide. The fabric section stretches about five blocks square. I thought it peculiar that there were a lot of dark colored lightweight wools. We were looking for scissors, yardstick, an iron, tape measures, and a bodkin to replace those lost in customs. We only found four pairs of scuffed scissors. We bought them.

Searching for scissors

Bill, being familiar with the market, got about thirty feet ahead of me. Perhaps you can see him in the picture. I did not want to lose sight of him.

If anyone has such items, please save them for the next trip. Notions are nonexistent here. Good cottons and linens are not available. Please save your items for us! Bill says that any items we can get to Melbourne, Florida, Missionary Flights International will bring to us when we are below the weight we are allowed. Would tape measures, metal rulers, an invisible zipper foot, and several rolls of Steam-a-Seam be too much to ask for?

Who donated the cardboard circles of straight pins with the big heads? They are great! How can we get more?

Bill bought diesel for the generator. We were the only customers. The two armed guards appeared bored.

Bill getting diesel for the generator. Note armed guards.

Bill getting diesel

A funeral service came down the street. The people were dressed in their best. The assortment of men's suits was interesting. None of the suits fit in quite the expected American way, but they were flashy. They march several people wide down the narrow streets, similar to the way funerals march down the streets in the French Quarter in New Orleans.

Church service this morning was inspiring. Pastor Lamb, perhaps you could use some of these ideas. There were two fans. Again, one was aimed at the pastor and one was aimed at us spoiled Americans. We sat on the first row on the narrow wooden planks that serve as pews at most churches here. The service begins at 10:00 AM with songs, choir specials, and announcements until 11:00 AM. We have another light bulb moment when we are recognized as visitors.

Then the sermon begins and lasts until noon. Some people sleep. Children wander in and out. A goat stuck his head in the side door by me and looked around, but decided not to enter. During the sermon I try to find words I recognize, which keeps me busy unless I am distracted. It seems there is always a lizard that climbs the wall directly behind the pastor. I guess that means there is a good chance one is climbing the wall beside me. Sometimes I recognize the songs enough to pick out a few Creole words, but by the looks I get I could be wrong.

Lest you think I am having way too much fun here, let me tell you about my private devotions.

No, they are way too rewarding also.

Pray for Kristy, who is doing my bills, and for Wes who is keeping it all together. Pray especially for each student I will contact, that each heart will be prepared to hear how God can give them eternal life.

Haiti Beauty Procedures

1. Choose a spot with the strongest light. The kitchen has a twenty-five watt bulb, so make full use of it.
2. Gather beauty products in one place. I take the complete two feet of kitchen countertop. I am worth it.
    a. Extra strong backwoods water-resistant eight-hour protection deet insect repellant spray
    b. Sunscreen. If you can find SPF 300, use it. I only have SPF 75. Look for oxybenzone at 2.0 and octinoxate at 7.5. Choose carefully. This doubles as your fragrance for the day.
3. Place your two-inch square mirror, if you are fortunate enough to have one, on the bottom shelf of the upper kitchen cabinet, which makes it about four feet from the floor. Bend over so you can see in the mirror, but do not back up, because there is a one inch drop in the floor right

there. The kitchen light is now behind your head. With practice, you can hold the mirror in your hand and face the kitchen light, but then you only have one hand available to apply your beauty products and earrings. You get to choose.
4. Apply skin care products (see 2a).
5. Apply beauty products (see 2b).
6. Put on earrings (see 3).

Bonus:
Entertainment Section

Things to do at night in Milot:

18

Monday, March 09, 2009

Greetings from the Lost Paradise!

We watched Glen Iris Sunday School of the Air Sunday morning and Sunday night service semi-live over the Internet. It was great to see the backs of your heads! The relay caused some strange still shots. We were pleased to see that you have reserved our places.

The Youngers watched it with us. Bill used some of Pastor Lamb's points in his discipleship group morning devotion this morning. Thank you, Pastor Lamb, for faithfully teaching and guiding us. This man is God's gracious gift to Glen Iris Baptist.

The ten-member medical team gets here tomorrow afternoon, bringing supplies and goodies that many of you collected and Lamar sent. It will be like Christmas. Thank you!

Remember when I asked you to think what you would do if you had no electricity, no telephones, no Internet, and no entertainment? Well, Sunday afternoon I was able to read and study all the Minor Prophets. I have wanted to do that for some time but just did not have time. Isn't God kind to give us what we need?

Speaking of public utilities (we weren't?), imagine again having no gas company, no electric company, no sewer or water company, no garbage pickup, few gas stations for your car gas, no Social Security, no unemployment benefits (thank you, God, for unemployment benefits), and no government benefits. You would not have flowing faucets, flushable toilets, bathroom plumbing, kitchen plumbing, perfect temperature and light control at your touch, or running cars. You would essentially be in Haiti.

Most families have many children. They are required to send them to grammar school through the sixth grade. Although public education is free, the cost is still quite high for Haitian families who are required to pay for uniforms, textbooks, supplies, and other items. Only 65% of primary school-aged children are actually enrolled. At the secondary level, the figure drops to around 20%. Less than 35% of those who enter will complete primary school. GMS, as a private school, is an exception and produces much better results.

If a family has a promising child, they will save to send that one to high school. If that one should graduate and get a job, he will provide for his parents in their old age unless he dies. Then the family plans are over. This is the Haitian retirement plan. This is much like the biblical plan.

Do you think your children would like this idea?

I treasure your words more than you could know.

Pray that we are able to price the items correctly, and that these people see only Jesus in me every time I am with them.

Lynda,

From the Land of Air-conditioning

Father, thank you for allowing me this blessing, for America, for Glen Iris Baptist Church, for the ROMEOs who meet at McDonald's, and for all my supportive friends and family. You give abundantly and without ceasing.

19

Monday, March 09, 2009

I am among the most fortunate of women in Haiti. Jack found a broken, triangle-shaped mirror roughly ten inches long on each side. Now I can see my hair to comb it. I will not be throwing away my faithful small mirror just in case.

And this makes it possible for me to send you ladies the promised beauty guide:

Hair Care
In the Lost Paradise
(Shampoo in a Pot)

1. Assemble pot and shampoo or soap. Yes, soap. Do not be picky.
2. Heat water in a large pot. Dilute the water with cold tap water for precise temperature control. See Shower in a Pot, Volume 1.)
3. Wet your hair in the sink or shower. Hold your breath and use cold tap water to save the precious hot water.
4. Frugally apply shampoo or soap and enjoy a luxurious massage.
5. Keeping your head over the sink, with your eyes closed to avoid the shampoo, feel around for the heavy pot of hot water. Carefully, without raising your head or opening your eyes, hold the pot full of hot water over your head and pour slowly: "dousman". This takes practice. I have not mastered it yet. If you go pour too quickly, you will still have soapy hair and no more warm water. Then you have to go back to step two. Ask me how I know.
6. Dry your hair with a towel or tick your head out of the door to hear if the generator is running. If it is, run back inside and quickly use your blow dryer with its expensive heating element. Blow your hair any which way to get it dry before the generator goes off.

7. Check out your new look in the new broken mirror if you are as fortunate as I am. What you see had better please you, because that is now your hair style.

Alternative Method
(use when generator is off)

1. Wash your hair at night in cold water.
2. Air and towel dry your hair as much as possible.
3. Sleep with damp hair.
4. Do not check yourself out in that mirror. Trust me. You have a unique, totally different hairstyle.

Now I'll tell you the really good stuff.

When I got to class today, the girls were subdued for the first time. Several hugged me. None were smiling. My interpreter FiFi said they had found out that today was my last day.

Surprised, I said, "It is?"

"Yes, we were told that," FiFi said.

When I finally got across to them that I would be here for several more weeks, they all laughed and hollered. Then we worked. Everyone grinned at me more than usually.

At the end of the class they asked me to step outside on the balcony. Because they thought it was my last day, they had gone in together to get me a gift. FiFi's husband had painted a picture of a Haitian daily scene for me. They had wrapped it carefully in a thin much-recycled scrap of ubiquitous black plastic.

I cried.

The students want a broom so they can sweep out the sewing room from now on.

Lynda

So blessed

Lord, thank you for these sweet students with their kind hearts. Your blessings are rich and undeserved. God, You are mighty and gracious to allow me this privilege. Please make me worthy of Your name. All the glory is Yours. Keep me in Your will. Thank you for my family, but mostly for providing a way we can go to heaven simply by accepting Jesus' payment for our sins.

20

Tuesday, March 10, 2009

Parable of the Lost Paradise

*O*nce upon a time there was a ruler with a vast kingdom. He created it with wisdom and with love. Abundant foliage and ample moisture assured good growth and crops. He set it apart on an island with beauty in its bones.

But all did not stay beautiful. The people voted to honor the witch doctors and Satan and called their worship voodoo. Slowly the beauty left the land. The water became polluted as they neglected sanitation. The very wind that the people breathed carried disease and worms. Their health began to leave. The blessings they had enjoyed began to disappear as they misused them and gave honor to the witch doctors rather than the ruler. The flowers and colorful birds disappeared. Most of the birds that remained resembled crows, and their sound was a gargling caw. The animals were sad and hungry. The people were discouraged and would not see why. Their money went to witch doctors and cell phones and survival. Their fears multiplied. Their jealousy increased as their hearts hardened.

Evil prevailed and the ruler was saddened.

But He allowed them their choices in His patience.

In His love and mercy He kept a presence in the land. He called forth keepers and witnesses from the Land of Air-conditioning to live out His truth among the people. They were to disciple and show by example. They worked loyally and tirelessly to show the love of the ruler.

The ruler rewarded them with contentment and eternal rewards.

I am a privileged princess in this land. I am in an isolated enclosure, prepared and maintained by others. Beyond the barred and locked gate, I see lost faces. Beyond my walled security, I see danger. Beyond the planted and tended garden, I see barrenness and hunger. Beyond my students' eagerness, I see little hope. Beyond my self-sufficiency, I see my need.

He looked beyond my faults and saw my needs.

> I, the Lord of snow and rain,
> I have borne My people's pain.
> I have wept for love of them.
> They turn away.
> I will break their hearts of stone,
> Give them hearts for love alone.
> I will give My life for them.
> Whom shall I send?*

A while ago the dogs found a man on the property stealing during the night. He ran away down the street, but the guards chased him and caught him. They brought him back and tied him to the big tree in the middle of the complex. The dogs were trying to attack him.

According to Haitian law, they should have legally killed him as he was on private property after dark uninvited. Evil is obviously suspected under those circumstances. Of course, Bill would not allow that.

They had gathered all the things he had stolen and placed them around him as proof before they called the police. In some cases the family is called to prove to them what the man has done and to shame him. The police took him away, but let him go shortly.

He returned later and stole the school's books.

Lynda,
From the Land of Air-conditioning

---

* Copyright Daniel L. Schutte. Used by permission.

21

Thursday, March 12, 2009

Whoever has been praying that I would lay off the e-mails, God heard your prayer. We have had no Internet service. This act of kindness could well be repeated, so bear with me.

The supplies came in! Thank you, Mr. and Mrs. Lyon, Wes, and all the others who rushed to gather items for the medical team to bring in. MFI originally said they were overweight and could not bring those items, but somehow that changed, and they were able to get them on board.

I felt like Elijah when God had his meals flown in via ravens as I opened all the great gifts. Listerine mouthwash! Dried fruits! Rulers! Lamar said he got a little happy when he was picking out items, and it showed. God is in the details. He uses His people.

Whoever chose the steam iron, it was a great choice. I am having trouble teaching the girls how to use it. They immediately pour the water out. They are only familiar with a hollowed-out metal container that they fill with hot charcoal (probably mahogany) for ironing. They wrap the handle with rags for protection from the heat.

Today I want to introduce you to my class. They are all in their early twenties or younger. Two say they can sew a little.

1. Martine is a statuesque, fashion model type. She is known for her Christian principles, and she is quiet.

Martine copying patterns

2. Mercilia is left-handed. That is shameful in this culture. She was struggling with cutting until I gave her our one pair of left-handed scissors. Did you donate them? You should have seen the delight on her face!

Mercillia is left-handed.

3. Elvie is the outstanding talent. She is a quick learner and the out-front top achiever in the class. She smiles all over.

Elvie enjoying class.

4. Denise wants perfection and tries hard for it. She is quite serious.
5. Inelia is a gorgeous cut-up. She tries hard and is outgoing. She also tries to get Luvrance to do her work for her.
6. Luvrance (roll the r) is determined and works at this. I want her to enjoy it more and not do Inelia's work.

Haiti: The Lost Paradise

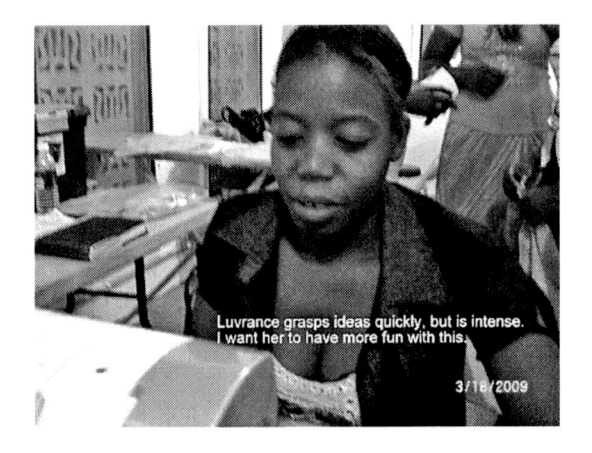

Luvrance is too serious to smile for me.

7. Bertha is shy, afraid to ask questions, and creative.
8. Claudette is extremely thin and shy. She likes color.
9. Raquel is shy. Her face is sculptured like a model's face.
10. Somira (roll the r) is a quick learner, impatient, and creative.
11. Chella is quiet and creative.
12. Suzanna is a beauty who loves short, tight skirts. She also changes her becoming hairstyle everyday.
13. Chedley is creative. She could be a fashion designer.
14. Marise has a low, melodious voice and smiles easily.

Sewing comes easily for Marise.

15. Yola is extremely shy and quiet.
16. Nola is the teacher I am training. She is slowly beginning to let me help her instead of seeing me as competition. I think.
17. FiFi is my interpreter. Pray for her. I keep her hopping and she still smiles!

Of these girls, the ones who need your prayers the most are Bertha, Claudette, Raquel, Marise, and Yola. These girls came in after the two-day cutoff for enrolling on the condition that Nola would work with them and bring them up to date. They entered the class on the fifth day. They are hopelessly behind. Each day they retreat more into their shells. The rest of the class is moving quickly, so these five girls are discouraged. I try to give them extra time, but that is difficult with so many that are enthusiastic and rushing ahead.

I am afraid that if I require them to drop out, they will be embarrassed in their group. Pray that God will guide me on this.

Now please attend class with me!

First, look into all the beautiful eyes and claim each girl for Christ. Pray. The girls will crowd up really close when you pray.

Enjoy this moment.

Next, start on today's devotion. Today we are discussing our talents. Who gives you talents? Why? In the parable in Matthew 25:14–30, why did each servant get a different number of talents? Do you have more or less than others? What does God expect you to do with what He gives you? How can you use your talents to reflect your relationship with God in your clothes?

My goal is to get them to see the connection between using their God-given talents and reflecting Him in how they dress.

We discussed clothing styles and how to choose your clothes to glorify God. In Haiti, a mark of feminine beauty is large hips, so they like to wear skin-tight skirts to show off their best feature. I told them that in America women often want smaller hips and try to put more emphasis on the upper part of the body. Judging from the incredulous looks I received, this was difficult for them to believe.

So far no one has taken her skirt in tighter than I had fitted her. One girl agreed to lower her hem line to the top of the knee. Suzanna did not lower hers. I know they can take them up at home after they have made them in class and modeled them in the fashion show, but they do not have the equipment we have. Thank each of you who made that happen.

I am trying to consider their culture and also encourage them to trust God's standards of modesty.

Next is review. Get those stickers ready! Start with the obvious questions so everyone will feel secure and confident, and then ask for conclusions so the advanced ones can shine. Be generous with the stickers. They love to see those colorful stickers adding up on the index cards with their names on them.

I love to see their names on the index cards, because in the flurry of the moment I can forget names.

Class is high energy and enthusiastic. When they have a problem, they are to raise their hand for me to come to them. If several have raised their hands and I am stopped with one student, they get impatient. It is not unusual to have a sea of several girls standing, waving wildly at me, hollering "Leenda," while I thread my way to them with FiFi a blur in my wake.

Look at the elastic this girl is using. It is wavy and has many colors. She says it has been in her family for a long time. Imagine that.

Lynda,
God's servant

Father, forgive me for not always appreciating the abundance I enjoy from You. Indeed, Father, sometimes I even forget these things are gifts. Thank You for reminding me.

22

Friday, March 13, 2009

Imagine you are a five-year-old child in Haiti. Your parents died or perhaps cannot afford food for you. There is no welfare, no child protection service, and no relative to help you.

If you are fortunate, a family will let you live with them and work for your keep. You may do the tasks family members do not want. You may scrub clothes with harsh detergent until your nail pads bleed and become hard. You may eat what they leave or do not want. You may walk to the well at Good Shepherd Ministry and carry home water in a pail on your head. A five-gallon bucket of water weighs about forty pounds. You may do the most menial and nasty jobs. If your new family is kind, they will allow you to go to the afternoon classes for indentured servants at Mission Bon Berger (GSM), but they aren't required to do so.

When you turn eighteen, you are on your own.

In a country with no social services this is actually a good solution.

You have found your life partner and you want to get married? First, according to Haitian custom, you must have a furnished house (one room with a place to sleep and minimal kitchen utensils—the kitchen is usually a grill outside) and a wedding dress or suit. Few have those items, so many of the Haitians just live together.

BeBe, an employee here, and his woman had nine children. His woman got sick and they were afraid she might die. BeBe says God convicted him to get married. So they did. The new wife got well. God teaches us to do His will in creative ways.

The medical team is here from America this week. They come about twice a year to check on the children in all three of the mission schools and give immunizations, worm treatments, and eye exams. Dr. Lynnette from Florida heads the group of volunteers from Alabama and San

Antonio, Texas. They have worked this week under the hardships of hot weather and long, difficult, dusty drives to the school's three campuses.

The medical team plus

Medical team leaving to work
Note mahogany trees in background

I picture God picking and choosing among His people to bring this diverse group of stars to this remote mission in Haiti. Hearing their stories around the dining tables in the evening before nightly devotions is a highlight of the day for me.

They entertained us in morning devotions with songs played on hand bells. Bill promptly named them the Dingalings.

Sandy came into class today to model the bias dress she made this weekend so the students could see the properties of bias. She was a great model.

Today in class we will trace off patterns and learn to read patterns. We had no paper for tracing, and the closest source is in Cap Haitien—an hour away. Christian drove all the way there and back to get it for us.

Last month at the Glen Iris Baptist School Homecoming, my seven-year-old granddaughter Cara won a crown for representing her division of the school. This was so unexpected that her surprise was obvious. Her eyes big, she kept telling me, "I won! I won!"

This was exactly how honored and unworthy I felt to be chosen to serve God here.

Lynda,

I won!

I won!

Thank you, Lord, for providing for our needs in unusual ways. Thank you, Father, because You let me win by coming here to experience again the joy of serving You.

23

Sunday, March 15, 2009

Yesterday was a day of tourist adventures for us.

We piled into the mission truck for the drive to the Citadel, the only tourist attraction here. I usually get to sit in the cab, which is a huge appreciated courtesy. The truck was outfitted with benches in the back today. Those in the back of the truck must contend with the rougher ride from driving slowly through the giant pits in the road, the relentless sun, and the constant dust.

The drive through all the rural neighborhoods and houses was fascinating. Few children wore clothes. A stream about four feet wide crossed under the road at one spot, and people were washing clothes, bodies, and dishes. Everyone stopped to watch us slowly drive past.

Every turn of the road revealed a new picturesque scene. There were giant trees with exposed gnarled roots clinging to the side of the road. Luxuriant self-planted ferns nestled against it. Here we saw a clean-swept yard with a leaning stick hut in the center. One could see between the sticks into the dark interior of the hut. Nude dusty children in the yard peered at us. Three chickens looked up as we passed. We are the curiosities here. There was a banana tree farm in a drop-off, a vertical wall of giant ferns, and a hut with blue tarps for a roof. The castle of a long-ago king could be glimpsed on a distant hill. It seemed incongruous with today's Haiti. Here the hillside dropped away to reveal a tiny dirt path connecting three huts in the valley. Everything has a fine coating of dust. My camera could not keep up. Bill said he would stop for me to take a picture, but there were too many perfect shots.

House of sticks for shade

Curiously, I did not see any farms or gardens except for the banana tree farm.

Some men jumped on the back of our truck to catch a ride. After the first few hitchhikers, our team in the back of the truck pushed them off. This was not cruel—if we had hit a bump, they would have fallen off.

Bill parked in the public area at the bottom of the steep walking trail to the fort. Vendors swarmed around us as if they smelled fresh American money. Several wore the red kerchief of the voodoo apprentices.

Vendors and Voodoo at parking area for El Citadel

About halfway up the one-hour walk to the top, the angle of the path became so steep we were gasping for breath. Our legs were aching from the unaccustomed stress. Haitians followed us in hopes they could help with a push from behind or by offering a donkey to rent.

The four of us who made it to the top first were smugly enjoying our victory when someone asked me if I had lost an earring. At almost that same moment, Steve from San Antonio, part of the medical team, walked up to me with the earring in his hand. He had found it on the trail. God cares about details.

Coming downhill, Bill showed us a shortcut. Have you ever seen any jungle adventure movies? The kind where you hang on to tree limbs and rocks to stall yourself from sliding straight to the bottom? Then you have a good idea of the descent. Mackenson, a GSM employee, stayed close behind me, ready to grab my arm if I should slide. I only lost my footing once (due to loose rocks), so I made a little better time than I should have.

Shortcut

On the road down, many who had seen us drive up were waiting to talk to us. One lady held her baby up to us. Bill asked us if we wanted a baby, because she had just offered hers to us.

Driving back through Milot, we paused by a card game happening beside the road because Bill knew some of the men. Every time one loses, he has to wear a clothespin on his face. One man was losing big time. He had six clothespins on each side of his face from his ears to his chin.

Off to the souvenir stands we went. This was a single row of attached huts with rented booths for the vendors to display their goods under the official sanction of the Haitian government. Most of the wooden carved items and paintings were similar from booth to booth. We were advised to barter. The vendors were so aggressive they would put items in your sack and expect you to pay for them. I got some jewelry made from coffee beans and colored berries, and some carved wooden vases.

They all say they have sick children, parents, and need money, and they are all hungry and this is their only way to get money.

We went to a French (yes, French) open-air restaurant with an ocean and garbage view beyond its enclosed security wall.. Bill parked in front in the roadside parking. There was a guard.

Cap Haitien beach and garbage view

They seated us at a table in a roofed area, set with white tablecloths, china, and glass goblets. With the missionary team we were fifteen. This felt like a banquet or a movie set. We were the only diners except for one couple. A small cat ran up a bush by our table to escape a dog.

We had a choice of beef, chicken, barbequed chicken, goat, steak, or shish kebab. Each choice cost fifteen dollars. Bill said the goat was good but had a lot of bones. I chose the chicken. Appetizers were fried bananas, rice, coleslaw with exceedingly hot sauce, toast triangles to feed perhaps half of us, and peanut butter sauce.

My chicken looked like a dwarf Cornish hen. It was served complete with the neck, tail, and a couple of other parts I did not recognize and did not care to ask about. The wings were about an inch long.

Oh, and we had a cola each. A treat!

The hostess showed us a room in the hotel. It had a standard double bed, a tiled bathroom, and blond furniture. It was about one hundred American dollars per night. The downstairs hotel rooms wrapped around three sides of a small pleasant landscaped area.

The property also had an ornate tiled swimming pool that had been used by the royalty who had the house built originally. It was still impressive after all these years.

When someone driving wants to pass you, they must honk because they could be on the left, right, or middle of the road and coming up on either side of you. There are no dividing lines in the road. Due to the deep ruts, a driver has to pick and choose where on the road he can drive. On the ten–mile, one-hour long federal highway drive to Cap Haitien, you might see eight other vehicles. The dust that they raise powders the spines of the cacti beside the road.

At night the cacophony of creative horn sounds are like a symphony by Mannheim Steamroller or some beginning, confused music group. You might hear a bicycle horn, a freight train blast, a diesel truck's low blare, a French police siren, an English police siren, ambulance horns from three different countries, a normal car horn, or an "ah-*ooo*-ga."

Friday I received a roll of meat-wrapping paper for the girls to use to copy skirt patterns for their first sewing project. Christian drove two hours to Cap Haitien to get it for me. I instructed the girls carefully on the correct way to trace, including all the notches and grain lines, and went to help a slower student.

That is when I made a big mistake.

When I looked across the room, my assistant teacher had stacked all the papers up and was cutting them all out at once, assembly-line style. I shouted for her to stop (kompe), but she kept cutting. I ran over there and placed my hand on her hand to get her to stop. That was my mistake. I had humiliated her in front of the students. I explained to her and the students that the purpose here was learning, not being fast. Each girl had to do her own work.

I will apologize to her on Monday for embarrassing her.

Lynda,
Humbled

24

Sunday, March 15, 2009

What a treat this day has been. Inno, the lady who helps in the kitchen, was having her granddaughter dedicated today and invited us to her church in Milot.

We still have not broken our rule that we do not attend a church that has traditional drum sets on the platform. These were bongos. They also had an electric piano, guitar, and a singer. Most of the musicians slept during the service. Did you know most of our hymns can be sung to a calypso beat? Ask me how I know.

Artificial flowers hung from the ceiling and on the walls. This seems to be common in all the churches we have visited.

They began the service at 10:00 AM, asked us all to stand to introduce us (again a light bulb moment), and began the singing. The preaching began at 11:30 AM and lasted until about 12:15 PM.

I have found it difficult to follow along when I can not understand the words. I wonder if that is how unsaved people sometimes feel when they hear a gospel message.

The preacher was animated, and even broke into song with a calypso beat. The offering plate is at the front under the pulpit. The people go up front to put money in. Martine, one of my students, was there. I felt so pleased to see her!

After the service, the whole truckload of fifteen of us threaded through the small, curvy lanes to Inno's house. Bill drove at a creeping pace through the narrow dusty trails. Clusters of huts and small houses grew close to the trail at every angle, respectfully following the natural contours of the land. This created a quaint, relaxed look. They obviously feel no need to disregard the natural shape of the land by scraping all the soil and vegetation off and leveling the soil. That must be an American thing.

We attracted a crowd. People stood by the road and gathered on their porches to watch us as we invaded their neighborhood.

We were invited into the front room (of three), where they had laid out a feast for us. The room was about fifteen feet square. The table in the middle took up most of the room so that no one could walk through the room once we were all in place. The ceiling was covered with red and white checked vinyl tablecloths and decorated with many strands of Christmas lights. Of course, they had no electricity. The neighbors brought in chairs for most of us.

Bill had told us earlier that we ate at our own risk. I hoped half a pimento cheese sandwich wouldn't be harmful, but I shared it with one of the medical team members just in case.

They also offered fried bananas, two sliced tomatoes, and about six pieces of lettuce, all artistically arranged. And they had bottled colas. We were told which one had alcohol.

We were careful to take little food, because what was leftover would be all their family of ten would have to eat.

Would we Americans be that hospitable?

I wandered outside so someone else could use my chair at the table. The family had new piglets in a fence that staggered down to the creek. Several women were washing clothes and children in the muddy creek. All was peaceful.

Dinner is ready. Please be patient because Internet service is skimpy and often disappears, taking my e-mail with it.

Lynda,
Not suffering for the Lord

25

Wednesday, March 18, 2009

Greetings from the Lost Paradise!

*L*ast night I had so many gnat bites that I woke myself up at dark thirty, clawing at my arms. I prayed myself back to sleep. This morning my arms had bruises.

Christian found a new source of meat-wrapping paper in Milot, only a quarter of a mile away. It is a great thrill for the girls to have their own paper patterns. One girl had a pattern catalog that was years out-of-date. They use this catalog as inspiration. A purchased twenty-dollar paper pattern would cost them about 160 Haitian dollars.

Inelia and Denise copying patterns

Bertha, Mercillia, Elvie, and Marise copying patterns

Christian showed us his two-story concrete house in downtown Milot. It is located two doors away from the main street at the intersection where a tire has been in the road since we were first here. His house is heavily decorated and protected with the iron work that he does so well.

Christian Levaux

Christian grew up as an orphan at Good Shepherd Ministry. He now has five children and raises three orphans. Because of his successful life and prosperity, some Haitians are jealous and envy him. Recently someone tried to kill two of his children by giving them candy laced with rat poison, or three-step. It is called three-step because a rat dies within three steps of eating it. Normally a child would eat such a rare candy treat immediately, but for some reason his children ran excitedly to show their Mother. She recognized what it was and prevented their deaths.

Christian did not allow this to intimidate him. He said it proves that God protected his family because He loves him.

Christian is an exception among Haitians. He understands that feeding and caring for your livestock is a smart business move. He has a man who drives his cows to good pasture every day, watches over them, and drives them back at night. It always makes me smile to see his big hefty cows lumbering down the main highway, boldly tattooed "Christian" on their sides.

Christian's cows going home

If a cow is stolen, killed, and eaten, it is difficult to prove ownership, so Christian's cows are protected overnight on the GSM property. When calves are born, Christian gets the first one. His worker gets the second. When the mission needs beef to feed the children at the summer Vacation Bible School, naturally they buy a cow from Christian. He is a sagacious businessman.

This morning in devotions we studied Isaiah 46 where God was angry because the people paid gold to have idols made that they had to carry around. The idols were burdens for their animals to carry. Those people had to care for their gods. God cares for us.

Joscelyn did a parody of this, mimicking how American teens saunter with their low-slung pants with no belts as if they were full of idols. Perhaps they are.

Joscelyn mimicking American teens

Bill once had the idea to have his son write a five-page Bible study on belts. Some interesting facts came up:

*Men are girded (belted) when they are prepared.
*Men are girded when they are going to war.
*Men are not girded when caught unaware.
*Men are not girded when they are rebellious.

During devotions I was distracted by footwear. Lamar, a GSM employee, wore bright pink flip-flops studded with huge rhinestones.

Did you not love the friendships and social times you enjoyed at school each day? It is the same here. The students wait for me in the shade of the high school's second-floor balcony. They do have to watch where they step, however, as Christian does let his cows and goats graze in the school yard.

What a treasured privilege it is to have time to spend hours reading the Bible. There always seem to be urgent things to do in America, so they get priority over the important. Here no telephone rings, no meetings are scheduled, no mail comes, no appointments need to be kept; there are no errands to run, no television or air-conditioning to anchor us to our homes, and no cars to transport us to McDonald's or somewhere else we do not even have to go. We all know how rewarding it is to spend time reading the Bible, but we still do not do it enough.

Lynda,
Deeply Blessed

Father, in Your great wisdom You have given me what I need and I thank You. You are Lord of the earth and Lord of the heavens, yet You love me enough to direct my footsteps daily. Please use the words You give me and my actions to turn others to You.

26

Thursday, March 19, 2009

This is for all you men.

How many business casual or knit polo shirts do you have with some company logo or name on them? How many do you actually wear? Have you ever wondered where they all go to die? They go to Haiti!

Charities and other businesses ship unsold merchandise to Haiti in large plastic bundles. These could contain clothing, cosmetics, food items, paper goods, or anything. The ships drop the bundles on the docks for the people to buy. That is what they sell to each other in their house front stores or in marketplaces. They call it *peypey*. (I am not sure how it is spelled.)

So the Haitians appear to be advertising American companies, rock groups, country clubs, sayings, or ideas on their clothes. It can send a confusing message. Obama shirts are abundant.

Classes are wonderful. God has blessed me with some of the best of the Haitian young girls. They have made four projects:

1. A tote bag to learn how to use the machine
2. A gathered skirt to learn how to use the serger
3. A bias skirt to learn how to use bias
4. A blouse with two different fabrics to learn how to accurately fit.

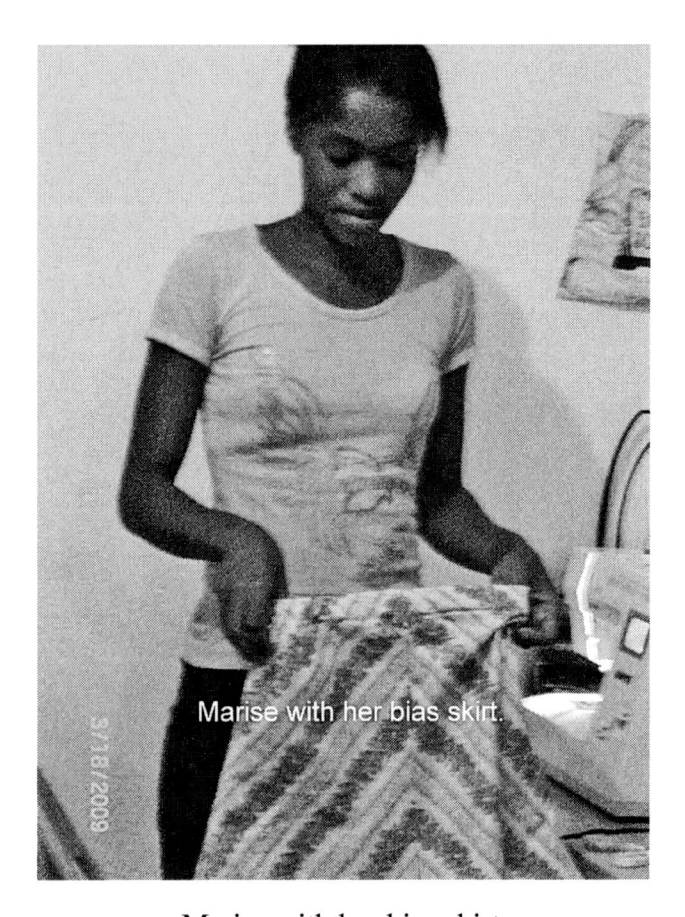

Marise with her bias skirt

Two girls are moving along so quickly that I am going to let them do a fitted skirt with a zipper. The fashion show should be spectacular! Most of these girls have never even owned more than three skirts.

Lynda,
God's woman in Haiti

27

Saturday, March 21, 2009

Bill and Sandy are exceptionally gracious. I see many serious and dramatic situations being played out here that require the wisdom of God, and they have it. Bill runs the mission with its giant payroll, giant potential, and giant problems totally through his dependence on God. They are always in the spotlight and always meet the challenges.

They have invited us over two times for movie nights. This involves opening our door, turning left, stepping over Bear sleeping, and walking about five steps to their back door. This was like a grown-up date night, and I loved it. We saw *John in Exile*, which moved me to tears. I ordered copies to be sent to my home address so we can share it with you. We also saw *Martin Luther*. Sandy served popcorn.

I cannot imagine how difficult it must be to live as publicly as Bill and Sandy do. God has chosen well to have them here. I have witnessed so many occasions where Bill met a challenge with discernment that had to come from God. This requires the dependence on God's leading that God expects of all of us.

Sandy and Bill

Bill excels in discipling people. God has given him great opportunities to practice his gift every morning at the devotions with the neighborhood men and daily with the GSM employees. After dinner at night he shares his thoughts and challenges individuals one-on-one.

When there is no team here, Sandy prepares all the meals. She fixes three full meals each day for us and does not seem to want help. She tells me when the generator will be on so I can do laundry. She has Inno available to clean our apartment. When I am too hesitant to call for Inno, Sandy will ask me if I want her to clean. I would like to take Inno home with me.

It appears they plan well so that the visitors they have invited to stay here are free to use their time, talent, and energies doing what God sent them to do.

Lynda,
Blessed and unworthy

28

Sunday, March 22, 2009

*H*ave you ever been in a new environment and found someone you knew? Remember how great it felt? That just happened to me.

Jack and I ventured outside the front gate to sit on the concrete benches over the drainage ditch, talk with our guards, and watch the people watch us. This is Main Street, Milot, Haiti—a third-world country. We are the odd ones. It was fascinating. Everyone noticed the blancs. Several stopped to talk to BeBe and to get a better look at us. Few here have cars, so foot traffic is heavy. No, not like at the Galleria mall in Hoover. It is more like downtown Birmingham on a Sunday afternoon, but friendlier.

After school traffic from GSM's gate
Bill, BeBe's wife, and BeBe

After school traffic from GSM's gate
West toward Milot

West from GSM's gate

Lumber delivery across from GSM

Mahogany lumber for sale

I was recognized! Martine, one of my students, was walking toward me and we were both thrilled to recognize each other. We hugged, held hands and jumped up and down like grammar-school children. What were the chances of my being recognized on a main Haitian street! It made me feel more like a resident than a visitor. Jack took a picture of us grinning.

I do not know what the reputation of Mission Bon Berger is in Milot, but from what I can see it is a shining example of Christianity in action. The educational standards are kept high. The grounds are well maintained. Order is kept. It is the only property I have seen that looks clean and prosperous by Haitian standards. There are vehicles here. There is a garden, shrubbery, grass, and gates with locks to protect God's property. Garbage does not stand in front of the property or inside it.

The employees are treated with respect. Medical needs are met. Christian discipleship and consistency are practiced. Efforts are toward "train up a child in the way he should go, and when he is old, he will not depart from it." (Proverb 22:6) The vocational schools that brought us here further this goal. Bill feels that the hope for the future of Haiti is in the children.

This is being achieved through dependence upon constant spiritual guidance. Bill and Sandy's challenges would stun most of us.

Across the street behind another guarded, locked gate is a tiny group of shops scattered down a crooked dirt lane. I bought some vases from a talented potter there. His kiln is out in the weeds. There is a woodworker with some fine furniture under his shed, and a welder making furniture and the bars that secure most of the windows and doors here. The welder uses sunglasses only; no special protection for his eyes and face. There is also a government school that looks abandoned, but lots of things do. And there is a small clinic that treats itches.

Men welding

I am told Brother Lamb will be coming this summer to preach as a Keswick speaker. May I stay?

We love you and thank you for your prayers for us and for Haiti.

Lynda,

Pray for the people

29

Monday, March 23, 2009

Suppose you got sick and had to go to a hospital here. That is not a good idea. Bill took a man to the local hospital for a bad cut on his hand. They did not have any sutures.

Remember the lady here with the facial cancer that has eaten away her face? She is in great pain. The hospital will not admit her because they have nothing to give her, and others need the bed. No one has morphine or heavy pain medication—not even the hospitals. Sandy is trying to come up with some kind of mosquito netting to give her some relief from the mosquitoes that cluster to feast on her raw skin.

When someone here dies and the family has no money, the dead one must be buried immediately by the family. The morgue has a daily charge that the family probably cannot afford.

When TiFre was in the hospital for his jaw cancer surgery, the nurses often neglected to give him any medication unless Dorothy was there to see that it was done. Sometimes it was only Tylenol. They did a second surgery on him that same week and used only a local anesthesia. Remember that Dorothy liquefied all his meals and took them to him because no meals are furnished.

I am remembering this because Beth, one of the Glen Iris Baptist Church members, is having serious back surgery tomorrow in America.

I am thankful for America's medical expertise and cleanliness. I am thankful that God allows us freedom to worship. I am thankful to have been born by God's grace in a country so richly blessed by Him. I am thankful that God continually blesses me undeservedly.

It seems that the Old Testament cities were often begun in praise and thanksgiving to God, and within about two hundred years their zeal had cooled to apathy or rejection. Pray for America to remember her Creator.

Please pray for Beth and her doctors.

Thank you for your many encouraging e-mails. Thank you for being patient with me by overlooking all the typos that are inevitable as I try to type on this eight inch keyboard by the light of one dim light bulb. I miss you all!

Lynda

Thank You, Lord, for Your amazing love.

30

Tuesday, March 24, 2009

*O*nce upon a time, a girl in the Lost Paradise knew her future. Her days would possibly consist of getting peypey, or sacks of castoffs from America, that she can sell in front of her house, doing the laundry for her family when the drainage ditch or creek is flowing, and hanging her laundry to dry over cacti beside the dusty road. If she were fortunate enough to have an animal to raise, it could be killed and cooked outside over charcoal (probably mahogany). She would have many children to insure her future. Church is a major part of her life—much like at GIB. Voices do not need musical instruments because they learn as youths to sing loudly and on key.

What else is there for her? There is no library, no higher education, no medical care for her family. She would not be able to develop her talents or hopes or intelligence. But within each girl there is that hope, that desire, that talent that yearns to be developed into satisfaction.

So God whispered into the minds of His people.

Consider the talents of the girls in my sewing class:

*Elvie is one of those girls. Her talent and gifts are astonishing, but the reality is that she has no way to expand her ideas or apply them.
*Color excites Suzanna—as do short skirts—but she does not yet know how to make color work.
*Luvrance grasps ideas quickly, and she has many ideas to see fulfilled. She seems too somber for her age.
*Martine, quiet and modest, only wants to use her talents to glorify God.
*Bertha is self-conscious. She does not know yet that God has given her great talent.
*Design intrigues Somira, but how can she make it a reality?
*Chedley is fascinated with ways to combine fabrics and colors creatively.

*Yola is quiet but cannot quit grinning when she sees what she can do.
*Mercilia is embarrassed to find she could create an attractive garment. She thought she had no talent.
*Inelia is only here for the fun. She has found out that she has to do her own work, and it is fun.
*Denise is afraid to try. The serger terrifies her. But look what she made!
*Marise with the deep voice cannot believe how easy this is.
*Raquel has found I will not let her go back to her old sewing habits because these are better.
*Chella was a wallflower who has come off the wall to become a dynamic designer.

They are all amazed at the quality of fabrics flown in by God, using his people in the Land of Air-conditioning. They learn rapidly and are surprised at themselves, sometimes breaking into delighted, rippling laughter. They learn to model for the first ever Milot fashion show. Daily they begin to blossom as they learn to use the talents God has given them.

Proverbs 31 becomes alive:

She seeketh wool and flax and worketh willingly with her hands. (Verse 13)
She girdeth her loins with strength, and strengtheneth her arms. (Verse 17)
She layeth her hands to the spindle, and her hands hold the distaff. (Verse 19)
She is not afraid of the snow for all of her household are clothed with scarlet. (Verse 21)
She maketh fine linen, and selleth it, and delivereth girdles unto the merchants. (Verse 24)
Strength and honor are her clothing; and she shall rejoice in time to come. (Verse 25)
Favor is deceitful, and beauty is vain, but a woman that feareth the Lord, she shall be praised. (Verse 30).

And God whispered into the ears of his people.

Perhaps there is a rewarding future for these girls in the Lost Paradise. Perhaps the prayers of God's people are bearing fruit. Perhaps God has always heard His people's cry. Perhaps God is being glorified in Haiti right now.

Lynda Criswell

And God is still whispering into the hearts of His people.

Give unto the Lord the glory due unto His name.
Psalm 29:2

Speak, for thy servant heareth. (I Samuel 3:10)

The computer class is having a competition project to design the advertisement for the debut of the Bon Berger Evangelistic School fashion show on April 3. Enthusiasm is high. It is a toss-up which class is having the most fun while learning. But Jack and I both win.

Two computerized sewing machines have had breakdowns that paralyzed them, but a rest restored them. We were warned that a computerized machine would not function well in this high humidity. But, thanks to those of you who responded to God's direction, we have been able to pull out the trusty mechanical Singers. I gave the girls a choice between their original, rested machines and the mechanical Singers. They both chose a Singer. They like the fill-in-place bobbin. Who wouldn't?

It is humbling that when we ask an innocent question (e.g., what does breadfruit taste like?), they seem to delight in supplying the answer for us immediately. Someone actually climbed one of those impossibly tall trees, brought down some breadfruit, and gave it to Nezzie to cook for us. Our intention was not that our every wish should be satisfied. We were embarrassed that they tried to do just that.

Now I know that breadfruit tastes similar to cheese-scalloped potatoes. I also know how considerate and polite these people are.

Giant breadfruit leaves

Breadfruit cut up

They say, "Do you want a picture of the school children? We will dismiss the whole high school and gather them for a group picture under the mountain and sing just for you." Or, "Do you need paper for pattern making? We will leave now to get it for you in Milot."

GSM high school

"…my God will supply all your needs according to His riches in glory…"
(Philippians 4:19)

How does He do this? He uses His people: you.

Lynda,
Who knows many of His people

31

Wednesday, March 25, 2009

There is a curious Haitian ritual that I have noticed, and now I know why they do it. People clap or wave vaguely at random times. Sometimes they wave abstractly to the side, or clap in front of themselves. Lately I have found myself doing that too. But I never seem to be able to actually kill any mosquitoes. Interestingly, some people say the mosquitoes do not bite them.

When I was five, one of the favorite games my sister Jean, my cousin Midgie, and I played was "count the cars." We lived on Huffman Road, a major highway then, and would stand by the front concrete block fence. Each of us picked a car manufacturer and counted how many cars of our chosen type drove by. They were older, so they got to pick first. They always picked Ford or Chevrolet. I never caught on why they always won.

If we played that game today in Haiti by our front gate, about a quarter of a mile from downtown Milot, we would only see about six vehicles per hour during the after-work rush hour. Usually one can see a *taptap* (a pickup truck, covered or not, for hire to carry an unlimited number of people—you tap twice when you want off), a couple of trucks too old for the make to be recognized, maybe twenty bicycles and five motorcycles, each carrying several people and their often cumbersome loads, and an old, leaning school bus with the name of some American school district still stenciled on its side. Last night, a car about eight years old stalled right down the road. Jack said it had a starter problem.

Taptap in front of GSM

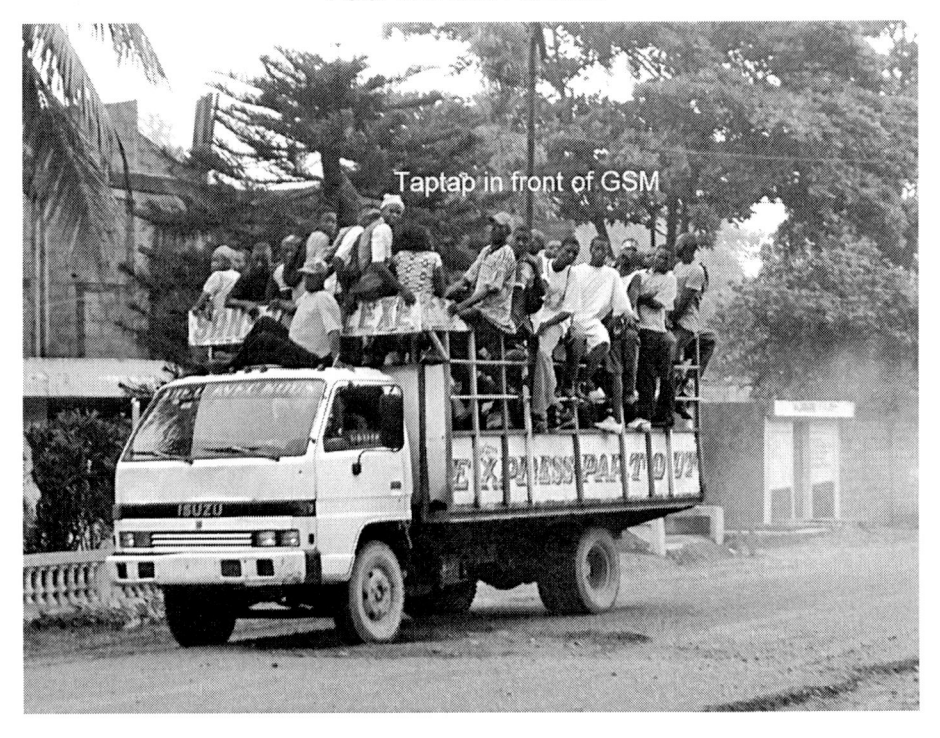

Taptap passing GSM's gate

There were also maybe twenty pedestrians walking home from work in Milot. I still do not think I could win.

Do you think you might want to be a missionary? See how you would handle the following kind of situation on a lonely mission field.

A stepmother, an employee of yours, does not approve of the boyfriend of her sixteen-year-old stepdaughter. The girl and her boyfriend go to a witch doctor to get her to change the stepmother's mind. He gives them a powder to sprinkle over the stepmother while she sleeps. The problem is that the girl can not figure out how to do that without her stepmother catching her, so she puts the powder into her coffee instead.

Within four hours the stepmother is dead. The boyfriend flees. Milot is angry. One of your trusted employees lies and tells the angry villagers that you caused it. The newly widowed husband tries to tell them that you were not involved at all, but no one believes him. The angry villagers decide to avenge the woman and begin to march to your mission to burn it down and kill you. The mob is within a block of your gate before your employee confesses that he lied and halts the disaster. He later asks for your forgiveness.

Do you still want to be a missionary?

Lynda
God's servant in Haiti

God, Your mercies are from everlasting to everlasting. Thank You for Your abundant blessings and protection.

32

Thursday, March 26, 2009

What do you know about demon possession? Americans seem to think it is harmless; it is make-believe or fantasy. It is alive and well in Haiti. Voodoo is the official religion of Haiti. The people periodically renew the contract signed with Satan two hundred years ago when they won their freedom from France.

There is a girl here whose mother was in voodoo. She is a pretty child. I helped her make herself four skirts. I noticed in the morning devotions that she did not want to touch her Bible. She has been known to attack and bite people. Her history includes some sad events.

One morning at breakfast she walked out of the room when Sandy asked her to do something minor. Then the girl began a high-pitched whining. Sandy sent her to her room because she knew what would happen next. Grown men could not hold this fifty-five pound girl to prevent her from hurting herself. She threw her clothes out her window. She tore up all her school books and threw them out the window. We were later told that she had previously destroyed everything in her room during these fits. She urinates on her mattress and all over the room. They try to make her safe until the attack is over.

This attack lasted six hours. She exhibited superhuman strength and endurance. I went into our apartment and prayed. The sounds that she made caused me to feel afraid for her.

The girl's grandmother has tried to control her in the past, as did her father. Neither could. She was banned from the school because she was so disruptive. Bill and Sandy have been trying to help her for eleven years. She knows she can break the power from Satan over her only by giving her life to Jesus, but she will not do it.

Someone who cannot live harmoniously with others is turned out to live on the streets. This is not necessarily cruel. The people share their food and look out for that person unless he becomes dangerous. If that ever happens, someone kills him. When a man raped a young girl, someone killed him that night.

Instant justice without the delays of a legal system can be quite a deterrent to crime.

The mission last year had an employee who was well loved. He disappeared and the mission tried to find him to be sure he was all right. He was located in a village where he lived on the streets. He sat and read his Bible in public daily and appeared to be doing no harm. The villagers were taking care of him.

Then there was a rumor that he died. Foul play was not suspected. Christian carried a picture of the man to the village to confirm that it was he, and it appears it was. The villagers had buried him.

Satan feels he reigns in Haiti. Perhaps he does for awhile. But our God is bigger and more powerful. He will always triumph over evil.

Pray for this girl and those like her, in America as well as in Haiti.

Lynda,

God's blessed servant

Several months later Bill told me that someone explained once again to this girl that God said His spirit would not always strive with us to bring us to salvation, and that this could be her last chance to accept Jesus. She decided to pray to accept Jesus into her heart.

The transformation was immediate. There have been no more episodes. Her attitude and even her voice have changed. Our God is patient and loving to draw us to Himself.

33

Friday, March 27, 2009

The class has begun practicing for the fashion show. I put a strip of yellow masking tape diagonally across the classroom floor as a guide for them to use to practice the fashion walk. We clap rhythmically to set the pace, singing a song in Creole with a regular strong beat, such as "Standing on the Promises."

Would you like to sing it?

>Si ou vle kase tout kod vie peche,
>Sin fos nan san Kris,
>Fos nan san Kris,
>Si ou vle vinke sou tout mechanste,
>Gin fos nan grou sil sakrifis.
>Alleleuia!
>Oui, gin fos, fos,
>Oui gin fos anpil,
>Nan san Kris krusifie,
>Oui, gin fos, fos,
>Oui gin fos anpil,
>Nan presiesan san Kris, Langno Bon-Dieu.
>(words copied from a book used in our morning devotions)

Doing the fashion walk does not come easily to them. They have a tendency to give a pronounced swing to their hips due to their culture. Often we all collapse into laughter at their fresh, enthusiastic efforts. The turn at the end of the tape is especially tricky for them to do correctly because of their natural inclination to project their hips.

Staging by dressing room

Chedley, Elvie, Luvrance, Lynda, and FiFi
In rehearsal

Luvrance practicing the runway walk

But the motivation is high. They seem eager to learn how to hold their hands and head gracefully and pose to showcase their garments. They practice repeatedly without complaint and watch me intently for correction and compliments. They have the great advantage of perfect, enviable posture due to balancing those huge loads on their heads.

We all laugh a lot.

We tried to practice outside the classroom on the balcony, but we gathered a crowd of curious spectators hoping for a sneak preview. The girls are not ready for public viewing yet.

Often I see a student shyly practicing by herself.

The Power of Scripture

A woman had just returned to her home from an evening of church services when she was startled by an intruder. She caught the man in the act of robbing her home of its valuables and yelled, "Stop! Acts 2:38!" (which says, "Repent and be baptized everyone of you, in the name of Jesus Christ for the remission of your sins.")

The burglar stopped in his tracks. The woman calmly called the police and explained what she had done. As the officer handcuffed the man to take him in, he asked the burglar, "Why did you just stand there? All the old lady did was yell a scripture at you."

"Scripture?" replied the burglar. "She said she had an ax and two '38s!"

Share this with someone who needs a laugh today and remember: The lady had confidence in her faith. It does not matter what the burglar heard!

34

Saturday, March 28, 2009

I actually know people in Haiti! We made the ten-mile, one-hour trip to Cap Haitien today for supplies and I saw two class members along the way. We all waved frantically. I can not explain how happy I was to see them. I will miss these girls greatly. Next week will be my last week with them.

Many of you know the rigors of this road trip. I left the truck seat so many times my lower back was raw from being scraped up and down. It was worse for Jack. He elected to ride standing in the back. Now he has an aura of dust and a newly sunburned face.

The market is always fascinating. There is an excitement in the air. Women strut around with wooden chairs threaded up their arms to display them for sale. Hats for sale are piled precariously high on the head of the seller. The bicycle shops display ancient cardboard boxes full of used greasy parts. Strings of warped shiny bicycle rims hang in rhythmic swoops in the air. Live chickens, swiveling their beady black eyes to look up at me, swing helplessly by their feet in the hands of their seller. A live chicken costs ten U.S. dollars. A chicken cleaned and cut into parts is eight U.S. dollars. The live chicken is more valuable because one gets the feathers and other vaguely useable parts. Vivid color is everywhere. Used, bent cardboard displays truly cheap jewelry for sale. Clothing is draped over walls, hung from anything, or multi-layered over the outstretched arms of the seller. Brightly colored and stark white polyester dress clothes are abundant. The styles look as if they were popular in the '70s. I saw a tailor's shop with a treasured old Singer machine proudly mounted in its warped wooden cabinet.

Bicycle parts shop

Live hens are $10

Lynda Criswell

Vendors with their portable stores

We have been warned that they expect you to buy anything you touch, so we do not touch. There is a slight omnipresent sour smell in the air. We walked quickly in single file behind Bill through the narrow streets. I wanted to look around, but had to watch where I stepped instead. And I certainly did not want to lose sight of Bill.

Next we went to a grocery store. It was about thirty square feet. There was an armed guard, with whom one checks any sacks or bundles. This was not Publix.

A container of liquid Tide at the store was 200 Haitian dollars, or over thirty U.S. dollars. At this time, the exchange rate was roughly seven or eight to one. One hundred gourdes equals $2.62 in American currency. It was a smaller sized container than the one I buy in America. There were only two containers of Tide on the shelf.

There was one package of Eight O'Clock Coffee, but there was a hole in it patched with tape. I saw a Publix juice bottle, but the lid was not screwed on tightly. The produce section had the familiar green cellophane-wrapped cardboard trays, but there was only one container with about ten shriveling strawberries, one with a green pepper, one with two cucumbers, and one with a few yellow squash. I bought a small tin of those cheap butter-like cookies marked fifty-two Haitian dollars, or over eight U.S. dollars. A box of eight marshmallow pies (not brand name) was twenty-two Haitian dollars, or over four U.S. dollars. A card table full of Valentine candy was on sale now, at the end of March. I saw a small chocolate egg for eight Haitian dollars. I may be having a junk food attack.

Jack had to direct Bill in maneuvering out of our parking space amidst all the people. This sight struck me as humerous.

Jack directing traffic

So many times I thank God for you.. Everything I do, everything I see, every new day brings reminders of how great God is to direct our lives to glorify Him. I do not take credit for any of these successes, because I recognize God's hand everywhere. This is an unexpected rich blessing that God has allowed me.

I am reading in II Kings now and see parallels in Haiti and America about the people repeating the cycles of obeying God and prospering and leaving God and being chastised. I hear witch doctors' drums at night. Their chanting is not the soothing melodious sound one hears coming from the churches; but strict, hard, monotone staccato beats. It seems an ominous warning.

TheChurchontheProperty practiced a song today accompanied by the slap-and-clap rhythm of the clapping games children in America do.

Jack and Bill worked all morning attaching a pump to the diesel fuel so Bill does not have to continue filling the generator the hard way.

Please pray for the fashion show on Thursday—that it will be a great outreach for God. We expect a crowd, and the gospel will be presented.

Thank you all.

Lynda,
Receiving God's blessings

35

Sunday, March 29, 2009

I found out that Haiti does indeed have tarantulas. Bill said the rain may be keeping them in hiding.

> …I will cause the showers to come down in his season; there shall be showers of blessings.
>
> Ezekiel 34:26

TheChurchontheProperty is in its seventh hour of services. It is now 1:50 PM. There have been cymbals, drums, electric organs, and multiple voices praying together. I did not hear an actual preacher. Their harmony is professional quality. They always sing a cappella and their many voices sound as one, even in four-part harmony. They have masterful control of their pitch and volume and are never even slightly off-key. The music weaves a peaceful calm and reverence into the background of my daily life.

FiFi has promised me my first motorcycle ride at 3:00 PM. It may be a short ride.

If you had never used an ironing board, would you know how to use it? The girls lay the garment on top of the board to press it, pressing in wrinkles on the bottom layer at the same time. I showed them how to slip the garment over the narrow end. They thought that was a brilliant idea.

The same God who heard the prayers of Abraham, Moses, and the apostles hears and answers our prayers in the same miraculous and wondrous way.

> "Thine, O Lord, is the greatness, and the power, and the glory, and the majesty"
> (II Chronicles 9:11).

Haiti: The Lost Paradise

Majesty!
Worship His majesty!
Jesus Who died
Now crucified
King of all kings!*

All we have to offer Him is already His.

Lynda,
His grateful servant

*Copyright 1981 Jack W. Hayford. Used by permission.

36

Monday, March 30, 2009

Greetings to ye in the Land of Insurance,
from God's lowliest of servants in Haiti

Bear lives here. His name is descriptive. He probably weighs more than I do, but neither of us is sharing that. His head is bigger than mine. When he stands, his head is higher than the arm of my chair. He is several shades of brown. I had not known a dog personally in many years until I met Bear. He works the night shift here with his mother, Luki, and they both sleep in the day. He is now sleeping under my chair. When he moves, my chair moves. When I first met him, he really liked me, but his infatuation has thankfully calmed down. When he walks, his back legs often try to pass his front legs. I have seen him sleep literally on his back with his legs up in the air.

Bear doing his job at the GMS front gate.

Bear working

Bear sleeping

The two of us are sitting on the concrete front porch under the shade of the large balcony on the top floor. I moved my white plastic chair away from the wall where Sandy killed two engorged ticks yesterday. When they first brought their dogs to Haiti, she said they got so many ticks that their ears were full of them. Now they get tick medicine to prevent that.

A breeze is blowing, the generator is purring, and my Bible is in my lap. I just finished reading. The huge almond trees and breadfruit trees and coconut and palm and grapefruit trees are moving in the breeze, casting lazy shadows over the freshly cut lawn. Air plants nest in the arms of the trees. Of the trees that have giant above-ground roots, strangely the longest, biggest root always points north.

I am being thankful for God's leading in my life. I think Bear is, too.

The baby of the lady with the facial cancer died on Friday. The family does not have five hundred Haitian dollars (eighty U.S. dollars) to pay for the burial.

Savanne Carre is the location of one of Good Shepherd Ministry's other schools. It is more isolated than GSM. They do not even have a generator for electricity. This is the location that has a witch doctor who lives next to the mission wall.

Bill and Sandy once spent the night there on the floor. Sandy said she felt her pant leg settle once, then again. She shook her leg to get the wrinkles out of the fabric. Then she felt two hairy legs touch her lower arm, and she screamed. By that time the tarantula was climbing the wall to return to his home in the ceiling rafters. There's a chilling thought. It was bigger than Bill's outstretched hand. He said he has seen tarantulas cross the road that were bigger than a box turtle.

He killed the tarantula. She did not sleep the rest of the night.

After hearing that story, I probably will not sleep, either.

One tarantula had a standoff with Bear the Great at the foot of the steps that go to the upstairs kitchen—right outside our apartment door. Cali, the cat, found one under those same stairs. In both cases, the pets had the intelligence to not attack the tarantulas.

Lamar did not tell me about this. It was not in any of the travel brochures either.

FiFi did not show up for my motorcycle ride. I figured either she did not want blood on her motorcycle, or she did not want to kill the American teacher.

Did you know that the fashion show is coming? Did you pray that God will be glorified? Thank you! Here is the verse that will be on their certificates:

> Give her of the fruit of her hands;
> and let her own work praise her in the gate.
> (Proverb 31:31)

The verse we used in class was, "Favor is deceitful, and beauty is vain, but a woman that feareth the Lord, she shall be praised." (Proverbs 31:30)

Lynda,

In the Lost Paradise

Please pray for the people.

37

Tuesday, March 31, 2009

Welcome back to my spot on the front porch! I was reading out there this morning when Joscelyn came to sit with me and keep me company.

Joscelyn has been on his own since he was five years old.

He tells me that when he was seven, his pastor told him God could not let sinners into His perfect heaven and explained that we are all sinners. The penalty for sin is death. Therefore, the only way we can go to heaven is if one who is sinless dies as our substitute. Jesus, the only sinless one, has done that for us. We only have to tell God that we believe what He said, and accept Jesus' sacrifice for us. Joscelyn did that and prayed to ask God to save him.

His goal became to get to America. He tried to leave Haiti when he was sixteen on a boat with many others, but they shipwrecked on Cuba. They were without food and water for several days. Most of them died. Cuba sent the survivors back to Haiti, but they were shipwrecked on Cuba again and returned to Haiti again. Haiti imprisoned the survivors until they promised not to do that again.

God sent Joscelyn to Bon Berger in 1974. He says he is like Jonah. Jonah tried to escape from God's plan for his life. God prepared a fish to swallow Jonah so Jonah would see God's sovereignty and concern for a heathen nation. This miracle also showed God's care and preservation of His own people.

Joscelyn feels that if he left Bon Berger, God would let him go to sleep. He says he works for God, not Bon Berger. He wants to reach witch doctors for God.

I shared with him how I first became interested in Bon Berger. Lamar Lyon, the GSM American representative, was organizing a mission trip at Glen Iris Baptist. Jack was going. I was not interested. During the last meeting, Lamar, who really did not know me at all, sat down by me and asked if I knew what the mission needed most. I did not know and did not care much. He just looked at me and said, "a sewing teacher." Lamar and the room seemed to fade away for me. I was vaguely aware of Lamar's mouth moving. I was greatly aware of God's presence and love and His inner voice saying to me, "All your life I have prepared you for this. All the sewing classes, all the training, all was for this."

I looked at Lamar and said, "Of course I will go."

I was naïve enough to think God prepared me to go to share with these people and bless them. Now I humbly realize that God intended this experience to enrich my life and draw me more to Him. Thank you, Father.

Joscelyn says we are a lot alike. I think he flatters me.

There is a series of four sewing classes I teach at Singer that I find particularly rewarding. Let me tell you about one last year that prepared me for where I am now.

Because so many teens cannot do simple math (like knowing what half of one inch is), I ask that students be sixteen or older. One lady registered her three daughters, and it bothered me that I forgot to ask their ages. I called her to verify and she said they were seventeen, eighteen, and nineteen years old. She did not mention that they were all special needs children. By the second class they were behind and discouraged. When I told the girls to put a tape measure around their hips, they just looked at me. Repeating the instructions got the same response: none.

The moment of understanding came to me when I reached under the cash register table to coax out one of the girls who was sitting on the floor crying. As I reached for her, I saw layers of dandruff and smelled strong body odor. My heart melted.

God was lovingly preparing me for a class full of students who wouldn't understand my words and did not have easy access to soap and water.

When you hug someone who does not get to bathe, you instantly smell the same way, so it does not matter anymore. God prepared me for this.

Then He sent Dorothy, author of the book on the Haitian language that Bill says is the best he has seen, to be at GSM exactly a full week before classes began to give me a basic emergency understanding of the language. He also sent FiFi to smooth the way during hectic class time. He had always seen my future needs and answered more generously and more creatively than I could have imagined. What a loving Father!

By the way, He has faithfully seen that every class has run smoothly to His glory.

I pray for you all that you will give your problems to God through His grace and trust Him with them.

Lynda,

God's humble servant in Haiti

Pray for the people.

38

Wednesday, April 01, 2009

A fifth grade teacher in a Christian school gave an assignment to her students to use common advertisements to describe God. Here are some of their results:

God is like Bayer aspirin. He works miracles.

God is like a Ford. He's got a better idea.

God is like Coke. He's the real thing.

God is like Hallmark Cards. He cares enough to send His very best.

God is like Tide. He gets the stains out that others leave behind.

God is like General Electric. He brings good things to life.

God is like Sears. He has everything.

God is like Alka-Seltzer. Try Him, you'll like Him.

God is like Scotch tape. You can not see Him, but you know He is there.

God is like Delta. He is ready when you are.

God is like Allstate. You're in good hands with Him.

God is like VO-5 Hairspray. He holds through all kinds of weather.

God is like Dial soap. Aren't you glad you have Him? Don't you wish everybody did?

God is like the U.S. Post Office. Neither rain, nor snow, nor sleet nor ice will keep Him from His appointed destination.

God is like Chevrolet. He is the heartbeat of America.

God is like Maxwell House. Good to the very last drop.

God is like Bounty. He is the quicker picker upper; He can handle the stains, and He will not fall apart on you.

This was e-mailed to me by my sister Margaret. I hope you enjoyed it.

Lynda,
Still laughing
Still blessed

39

Thursday, April 02, 2009

To my friends in the Land of Privilege:
You should see what a great job Jack's computer class did on the fashion show flyer! He gave them the necessary facts—who, what, when, where—and clip art. Keep in mind that computers and advertising and clip art are new to these men. They do not see the polished marketing examples we do, and they have only been learning for four weeks. This was the first project that they could design by themselves as opposed to a classroom requirement. The clip art was impressively and artistically arranged. One of my favorites started with these appropriate descriptive words centered:

flash flash flash

One of you sent fifteen tiny pink bows. Guess how many we needed for the diplomas? Don't you just love how God does that? And He does it, of course, before we even see the need. Many times I pulled out some trim or ribbon for a girl's project and found exactly the amount or the color she needed. Thank you for your obedience to Him. By the way, those of you who sent ribbon, laces, and small items in zipper storage bags, thank you! They are so much easier to access and see.

This fashion show tomorrow may require much prayer. Some of the girls thought they would be allowed to be in the show even if they had not completed the requirements: garments made *in* the class, index cards filled out describing each garment, all rehearsals attended, today's dress rehearsal absolutely required. One girl attended class about five days total and did not attend any of the runway practices. My previous supervisors (thank you, Mrs. Adams) taught me well: "no workee, no playee."

It is strange in this land of quietness (no electricity, no televisions, no humming air-conditioning units, and few cars) to hear the whapwhapwhap of a very low-flying United Nations helicopter directly overhead. Sitting on the front porch, I met the eyes of the pilots. They looked American. Their automatic weapons were drawn as they panned over the land. And me. Echoes from World War II? Forecast of the Tribulation? Just a United Nations helicopter?

Lynda,
God's lowliest servant

    Lord, You have made us to have dominion over the works of Thy hands. Please make our ways straight before Your eyes. Thank You for planting us by the rivers of water, not so we will just grow, but so that we will bear fruit. We stand in awe of You.

40

Friday, April 03, 2009

A time to sew (Ecclesiastes 3:7)

Byen Vini pou premye parad de Bon Bege!
Welcome to the First Ever Fashion show at Bon Berger!

Bel fanm pa di bon madamn pou sa,
Bel figi pa la pou lontan.
Men, y'a fe lwanj yon fanmm
ki gen krentif pou Senye a.

Favor is deceitful
and beauty is vain,
But a woman that feareth the Lord,
she shall be praised.

Excitement! God was praised and glorified in song, in prayer, and in the talents of the 2008 first ever graduating class of Bon Berger's Technical School of Sewing and Computers!

Ba li sa ki poul li a.
Le y'a we sa l fe,
Se pou tout moun fe lwanj li.

Give her of the fruits of her hands;
And let her own works praise her
In the gate!
(Proverbs 31:31

We've come a long way from Genesis 3:7 where it is written "...and they sewed fig leaves together." The girls easily stole all the attention away from the men's computer class graduation. Attendance was about sixty people, because there was a funeral in town at the same time, but enthusiasm and tension were high. One girl told me that the people wanted to come to the show, but the funeral had food and Coke, and we did not. Bill said she was joking.

As 1 Timothy 6: 8 says, "having food and raiment, let us be therewith content." (Sorry, Pastor Lamb, for the out-of-context quotes.)

Thank you all for praying, because your prayers were answered. This was a huge success! The girls walked the runway for over an hour, and we had songs and prayer and laughter. The community seemed surprised by their girls' abilities.

One shy girl, maybe fourteen years old, came up to me and explained that her mother and father died and she lived with Elvie (the extremely talented one). This situation is common. She said Elvie loves me, so she did, also.

Another young girl stood by me and watched me before the show. I asked her if she was enjoying the show, but she did not answer. I asked if she wanted to sit down, but still no answer. I told her she could stand there if she liked. She did not answer. She stayed by me through most of the show, watching me. Afterward she came up again. She did not speak or smile. Eventually, she walked away, looking at me sadly over her shoulder. I must be even more of an oddity than I thought.

The students enjoyed the rush of the timing to change between runway walks, the confidence of knowing how to walk properly on a fashion runway, the thrill of being able to make so many garments using all new techniques, and the astonishment that they could do something so professional. As with any group, we had last minute panics, missing accessories, and unexpected calls of nature, but no surprises.

Well, maybe one surprise. Ask me about Claudette's shirt. She is on the far right in the finale if you look at the pictures (and please do look). Remember that she does not know English.

The diplomas had a tiny pink bow at the top and had a color photo of each girl attached to the diploma with a colored paper clip. (Thanks to Lamar, the photos got here Tuesday.) Those paper clips were treasured. I saw one girl searching the grass for her lost clip. I saw several girls touch their photos carefully in awe. Yes, there were many tears and much laughter. Surprisingly, there were many wolf calls from the audience—

including the local pastors! We were told that was not unusual. The men here are quite proud of their women and they are vocal.

Hilaire, from Jack's computer class, was stationed on the balcony outside my classroom overlooking the fashion show and operated Jack's tiny computer that controlled the downloaded music. The small speakers were placed on the balcony rail and aimed at the audience. He was obviously enjoying the music himself. Jack spent much time getting this important part of the afternoon working smoothly.

Hilaire oversaw our music.

I did the welcoming speech in Haitian, as printed above. I hope that is what I said. I told each girl separately, "Bondyeu beni ou," and hoped I said "God bless you."

Lynda giving the welcome in Haitian.

Elvie made her skirt and her bag.

Denise made her bias skirt.

Lynda Criswell

Suzanna made her fitted skirt.

Marise made her fitted skirt.

Yola made her bias skirt.

Somira made her fitted skirt.

Chedley made her top.

Claudette made her fitted skirt.
Remember that she doesn't know English.

    My class secretly collected money to get a precious gift for me. It was wrapped, not in the thin black plastic bag that is ubiquitous here, but in heavy duty blue Christmas paper with silver snowflakes on it. It had been reused so often that the paper was uniformly wrinkled, thin in spots and taped repeatedly. I will bring it home.

The wrapped gift from the students.

We gave Birmingham T-shirts to Hilaire, Guy, BeBe, and others who helped as thank-you gifts.

Guy and Hilaire and their thank-you shirts.

Diplomas for the Computer Class
Jack, Toto, Gourneau, Guy, and Hilaire

The mission is only allowed two gigabytes of bandwidth per week of download volume, so I will not send photos.

His presence was with us or we could have done nothing. Thanks to each of you! You all had a part in this!

Lynda,

Extremely happy

Still not suffering

Note: After sending this e-mail, I posted this page in a popular sewing Web site where I had previously posted some of the needs for the mission sewing school. Many women on that site had sent items and asked great questions. However, when I posted a copy of this page so they could see the spectacular results, the administrator removed my post and said it was offensive to atheists and Muslims because I mentioned God and prayer. Only in America.

Lynda Criswell

The First Ever Fashion Show Finale
Bon Berger Mission

41

Saturday, April 4, 2009

Bill has come up with a facetious idea to multiply missionary support funds. Someone could develop the barren hill behind Bon Berger and build the expected and predictable primitive stick-and-stucco huts all along a winding dirt path up that hill through planted luxuriant tropical foliage. The inside of each hut would be equipped with air conditioning, luxury bathrooms and high-count linens on fluffy down bedding, shiny white stone flooring, discrete microwave ovens in the kitchenette, and elegant but rugged carved furniture. A secluded restaurant nearby would serve tropical fruits, exotic meats, and salads imported from America. There would be an extra charge for the exciting primitive hour ride from the airport to this remote area. For another extra charge, you could take them on day excursions to see cocoa beans processed, or people welding without protective eyewear.

Think, "Look, De plane! De plane!"

There is a church in Cap Haitien whose members are going around Haiti praying for others. We heard them singing and praying last night and today. This is a twenty-four-hour ministry. What a touching, tender call to our need of revival.

Jack has lost twenty pounds. The weather is perfect. The shrubbery is luxuriant. Jack and Bill have been working on improving the solar heater all morning, and the showers are hot. We love the people. The dogs know us. James brought us bananas. I hung fresh laundry out on the line. I have a full can of Baygon. My hair has become curly. My bills are being paid without me. I had fresh coconut for lunch.

What is all this about suffering for the Lord?

Lynda,
The blessed
Still not suffering

42

Saturday, April 04, 2009

The garden at the Good Shepherd Ministry's Savonne Carre campus was beautiful. We went today because Bill had a meeting there. It is their first garden, and the students are managing it. One student gave me a giant hot pink hibiscus bloom that I put behind my ear. They proudly shared lettuce, tomatoes, and carrots with us. Their cucumbers were huge and beginning to rot, so they did not share them with us. Bill found out they did not know what they were, and they did not know how to prepare them, so they just kept letting them grow.

GSM's campus at Savonne Carre

Lynda, Sandy, and Bill in GSM truck

I saw a large lizard today outside my classroom. Most of the chameleons I see here are similar to those we have at home. This one had a body the size of my hand. He was chocolate brown with stripes of tan and blue down his back.

Since my classes are over now, I am using some of my time to type the computer lessons for Jack. He can edit them and get them translated into French, the official language of the school.

This is my last Saturday here.

Lynda,

God's willing servant

Pray for the people.

43

Sunday, April 05, 2009

Greetings from the lost paradise!

You would think that by now I wouldn't have much to say. Think again. How wishful of you!

Today Jack and I visited TheChurchontheProperty. All the Sunday schools meet in the sanctuary, which is about the size of the GIB sanctuary, except that is their whole church. All of the people are in the same room, with nine Sunday school classes going on at once in different parts of the room at the same time.

Several people from our daily devotional group were there. BeBe looked especially nice today in his suit jacket. It looked freshly washed. Yes, I said washed. He sat by me. I found out later that he was assigned to me. Lamar and AuRel were also there. Hilaire from Jack's computer class led the singing. Guy, who was the emcee at the fashion show and was a student in Jack's computer class, led the prayers and did the announcements. FiFi met us at the door, walked us to the front, and sat with us until she had to leave for the choir.

You ushers should never underestimate how important your services are to visitors. It helps to be greeted.

The music director was a little (okay, a lot) more animated than we are accustomed to. FiFi lead a tremendous choir special. Most of the church singing was a cappella and reverent and professional in quality. The voices blended so well that each part sounded like one voice.

During one choir special, a child about two years old toddled up the platform. Someone helped her up, and she went to sit with her mommy in the choir. Later her daddy walked up and handed her mommy a juice bottle.

This was Palm Sunday. FiFi translated for me. The pastor explained what it meant when the people called out Hosanna, and how one can worship Him best by giving Him your heart.

The man in front of me was wearing a tan dress shirt. On the back of his collar the fabric had worn away, exposing an area of interfacing about half an inch by four inches.

Several men were wearing worn dress clothes that almost fit and sandals or flip-flops. Some of the dress shoes were worn like houseshoes, with the heel of the foot smashing down the back of the shoe. Most women were wearing polyester dresses with hose and heels or flip flops. Women here often leave their skirts partially unzipped. Several had lace on top of their head. Children were dressed in fancy Easter-like dress outfits. Everyone looked clean and happy. The drummer on the stage napped.

There was one electrical outlet. It was located in front of and directly beneath the pulpit. People charged their cell phones there during the service.

I still love the part where the pastor says a few words, someone stands up, everyone applauds, then he says a few more words, someone else stands up, and then you realize they are welcoming visitors. By then he is looking at you expectantly. BeBe motioned for us to stand. They always know we are visitors. It is yet another wonderful lightbulb moment.

We had visitors today at the compound. Hilaire brought his attractive wife to meet us. What a treat. I wished I had something to serve them, but I did not. Lack of a common language resulted in many awkward silent moments, but we shared big grins.

FiFi gave me my first motorcycle ride in the grassy area in front of the vocational school this afternoon. It wasn't nearly as exciting as it looks. I will stick with my car.

Motorcycle ride with FiFi.

My first motorcycle ride
FiFi and Lynda

    Do you remember the girl I told you about who kept watching me at the fashion show? She appeared at our gate Saturday. She was probably between fourteen and sixteen years old. She was wearing the same dirty sleeveless shirt she wore at the fashion show. It was too small for her and stretched out of shape to the point of being immodest. She probably does not have another shirt. Sandy and I were outside my apartment door talking when I saw her. She waved, we waved, and she stayed there. After a few more exchanged waves and about thirty minutes, we decided to walk over there to see if she needed help. The girl never smiled. There were tears in her eyes. Sandy asked her what she needed. She did not say anything, but kept looking at me. She finally said she lives with her mother's sister or her sister. Her parents are dead, which is common here.

Still no smile. When Sandy verified that she was not sick or hungry, there was nothing we could do.

We called for Christian to come with his good command of the Haitian language. She told him that she wanted to live here. Sandy explained that she could not do that. Christian explained that, too. She just kept looking inside the gates and at me. All she would say was, "I want to live with you." Eventually we waved good-bye.

She stayed there silently for over an hour, holding the padlocked gate.

After she left, I went outside the gates to look back in to see what she saw. I saw safety, peace, beauty, calm, protection, cleanliness, plentiful and safe food, water, a truck—all things we can enjoy every day in America. I took a picture through the locked gate.

Main house through gates.
Our apartment is on bottom left.

Main house through the locked gates

Jack said he saw her later hiding in the empty high school classrooms. Bill had noticed, too.

There are hundreds like her.

Sandy and I have set up a sewing factory in the dining room where we are making clothes assembly-line style. She cuts, I sew. I hope she is enjoying it as much as I.

This is my last Sunday here.

It is considered a sign of prosperity in Haiti for a man to have a fat wife because it shows he is wealthy. Bill said he did not know that when he met Christian's wife. Someone told Bill that Christian had the fattest wife of all. Bill said he thought at the time, "You creep."

I am beginning to like the smell of Baygon (Raid).

> Blessed be the Lord, who daily loadeth us with benefits.
> (Psalm 68:19)

Lynda,
The mouth of Haiti
An undeserving grateful servant

44

Monday, April 06, 2009

*D*id you know that a girl can dry her hair using an oscillating fan? Ask me how I know.

Cynthia tells me my yard at home is in full glorious bloom, but there are three cats in my house who apparently have forgotten how to use a litter box.

Here is an oddity for you. Most people here do not have window glass, only screens and bars. What music would you expect to hear coming from their houses as you sit in the devotional room? Would you guess French opera first or last? Make it your first guess.

Picture a second-floor room with a concrete roof, concrete floors, and concrete walls. The ubiquitous screened windows are on three sides. There is a door to the south leading out to the concrete roof of the room below, as well an entry door to the north from the upstairs hall and adjacent computer room.

This room is currently used only for our daily devotions at 6:30 AM. There are folding metal chairs all the way around the perimeter of the room, a table in the middle for the song books, and a permanent flower arrangement; nothing else—no lightbulbs, no pictures, and no curtains. Add a swarm of hungry mosquitoes.

The song books are printed in Creole and French words without music. They are color coded so one knows which section to use. This was an excellent opportunity for me to learn more Haitian words, as I often recognized the melodies. The bindings are loose, so we were careful to keep the pages together. They are stored locked in the computer room across the hall. Joscelyn sets the tempo by snapping his fingers.

We sit in exactly the same order every day, just as you do in your church. The regulars are Ronnie, Lamar (with the hot pink rhinestone flip-flops), Mackenson, BeBe, Joscelyn, Roland, Bill, Sandy, Aimee, me, Jack, AuRel, a second Lamar, Danny, Nezzie, and Inno.

AuRel is over 80 years old. He walks a half mile each way daily to attend morning devotion.

We sing two songs, pray, read the next chapter in the Bible, and the men ask Bill questions about the chapter. Often Bear tries to sneak in by lowering his head and walking slowly. His nails click on the hard concrete floor. Sandy always makes him leave. We sing another song and have a benediction.

Then, beginning at the person seated closest to the door, each one shakes hands and hugs the next one and moves down the line. The one next to him folds himself in line behind him, and so on until everyone has touched and said "Bonjou!" Beautiful.

Devotional group

Joscelyn brought his guitar to devotions Sunday and sang a song he wrote. Imagine a soft, wandering, wistful melody being sung reverently, almost whispered, by a humble, intelligent, wise man in Milot, Haiti, in that upstairs room and read these words:

> If you want peace, come to Jesus.
> If you want joy, come to Jesus…

The sincerity in his dark brown eyes was truly humbling.

My classroom has become my private place to worship God. I cannot go into that room without feeling His love and His closeness. The first day I went there, I dedicated it to God and asked Him to glorify Himself within those walls and to use every piece of equipment in it, including me, to show His love and glory. Each day when I go up there, I repeat that prayer and usually cry.

I wrote on an index card the date that the room was dedicated to God, and taped it beside the light switch as a testimony.

He gives me words to praise and worship Him and tells me who and what to pray for. Often He brings one of you to my mind. Often it is one of my students that weighs on my mind, or a situation that needs His care. He reminds me of His greatness and His love.

This is my last Monday here.

He shows me Psalm 56:13: "For thou hast delivered my soul from death: wilt thou not deliver my feet from falling..." (Most of you know I have no arches—and a poor sense of humor.)

> Whom shall I send?
> (Isaiah 6:8)

Lynda,

God's lowliest servant in Haiti.

Pray for the people.

45

Tuesday, April 07, 2009

Greetings to all of you in the Land of Excess!

This is my last Tuesday in Haiti.

Have you noticed that when you go to other countries, you want to try out their native clothing? In Hawaii you may want a grass skirt; in Williamsburg, a colonial outfit.

This is not a temptation in Haiti. If you support Hannah Home or Goodwill or similar charities by donating your clothing, you may see your donated clothes hanging on a dry, dusty cactus.

Forget Not all His Benefits
(Psalm 103:2)

The adults here call me Miz Jack. My students called me Leenda. Loudly. I call myself extremely blessed.

Do you know what well water does to your hair? I do.
Do you know what well water does to your teeth? I do.
Do you know that the people in the concrete devotion room pray for America? Think about that.

God Bless America Again.

My thoughts continue to return to the girl at the gate, looking through the rusty bars and padlock. Can you imagine what she must have been thinking or hoping? But I am inside. I get to live here. Thank you, God.

Most Haitians have never been outside of Haiti. Christian went to America once—Florida and New York, even! He thought it was a good idea that America drivers drive only on the right side of the road, not anywhere they please. He did not want to try the stairs that moved. He tried to bargain with the checkout clerk at Wal-mart to get a better price. That is how it is done here. He felt more confident at a pawn shop, where he could bargain.

He prays for America. He understands that all of us are sinners and deserve the penalty of death. Jesus paid our debt by dying in our place. You can receive God's gift of eternal life by asking Him to forgive your sins in the name of Jesus, and believing in your heart that God raised Jesus from the dead. Then you, like Christian, will have God's gift of eternal life.

Do you believe what God said?

"If thou shalt confess with thy mouth the Lord Jesus, and shalt believe in thine heart that God hath raised him from the dead, thou shalt be saved." (Romans 10:9)

Ask Him to give you eternal life.

"Our days are like grass ..." (Psalm 103:5)

Lynda,
God's servant in Haiti

46

Wednesday, April 8, 2009

The RahRah parades come down the street several times a week. Here they come now in front of our gates in a downpour of rain.

Would Christians be so dedicated? So loyal?

They have discordant instruments, disorderly crowds, suggestive dancing, whips, and defiant, angry looks. They shout. They look in through our barred and locked gates and can see me sitting on the front porch with my Bible. Today they carry a red and white flag with a goat logo; a red, white, and royal blue striped flag; a green and white flag; and a red, yellow, and green flag. I do not know if the flags mean anything, or they just found them. There is also a flag for the Queen of Africa. They worship her, too.

Voodoo people have a giant celebration here in protest of Easter, so the parades are more frequent now.

Sounds I can hear now:

voodoo band returning from Milot, approaching our gate again
children playing in the light rain
vehicle horn like a freight train
soft raindrops on giant breadfruit leaves
public taptap vibrating with Haitian voices
rain gurgling down the downspouts
Bear protesting either rain, voodoo parades, or something only dogs know about

All the dogs here look alike. There are no thoroughbreds, so due to interbreeding they are about the same size and all about the same color as the dirt road they walk on. Cats are very small, perhaps six pounds?

In the cities and on the rural roads you see handpainted signs everywhere on crooked weathered boards or walls advertising legal gambling. Bill said he once approached a group of men intently gambling. He asked if any of them had ever won. They all said no. He asked if any of them even knew anyone who had won. They considered this carefully. No, no one even knew anyone who had won. The apparent conclusion escaped them.

This morning Jack helped Bill and Mackenson, a GSM employee, dig a ditch. It will contain the pipe that will carry the shower water from behind the main house to the giant concrete drainage ditch that lines the street. Now the backyard will not bubble up when a team uses the showers.

Jack, Bill, and Mackinson working on drainage

I am leaving tomorrow. This is my last Wednesday here. I am moved to tears. How can I leave these precious people God has allowed me to meet and love?

By Missionary Flights International! I am fortunate that I have precious family and people (you) at home who God has allowed me to know and love.

Lynda,
Understandably sad

47

Wednesday, April 08, 2009

Greetings
to the people in the
Land of Air-conditioning, Insurance, and Excess

This is my last full day in Haiti. My heart aches.
 I can find no more excuses to be in my classroom. This is my last time to straighten it, clean it, and pray over it. I slip the red ribbon with its dangling key to the room's padlock off my left wrist. I have worn it almost daily for over a month. I will turn it in to Bill today.
 Thank you, God, for every second here.
 A volunteer American doctor working in a hospital here tells us about a lady that came in who was in labor. He could find no vital signs for the baby. He had no intravenous supplies, no monitoring equipment, and no medicines or pain relievers. He could not get her a bed because there is always a fee, and she had no money. It was a difficult delivery, but the baby was alive. In the afternoon, he sent them both home but told the mother to bring the baby back the next day because the delivery was so difficult. She did.
 He found out later that she walked three hours each way to get to the hospital: three hours home after a difficult delivery, and six hours to the hospital and back the next day.
 He wears flip-flops.
 You can not ask a patient if he has a fever, because no one has a thermometer. You can not ask their address, because most of the streets are not named.
 God has added to my vocabulary here. I can say:

  Alle   Go
  Rete   Reverse, back up

Haiti: The Lost Paradise

Kompe	Stop
Dwat	straight
Fil	thread
Egwi	needle
Koud	sew
Twal	fabric
Len	linen
Bobin	bobbin
Machin	machine
Gade'm	Look at me
Dousman	slowly, gently
Valise	purse, tote
Mash	straps
It, vit	hurry, hurry

I could get a job as a parking lot attendant or a driving instructor with the first few words! The rest are all terms that surely will be valuable to me at Singer.

Jack saw a "timeshare" earring. One fellow walked up to another, removed the earring from his ear, and put it in his own ear.

Today's Diet Tip

When thou sittest to eat with a ruler, consider diligently what is before thee: and put a knife to thy throat if thou be a man given to appetite. (Proverb 23:1)

Who can:

*hang the world upon nothing? (Job 26:7)

*lay the foundation of the world? (Job 38:4)

*provide for the raven his food? (Job 38:41)

*give a horse strength, yet make him afraid of a grasshopper? (Job 39:19-20)

*know the treasures of snow and hail? (Job 38:22)

*part the light? (Genesis 1:4)

*beget drops of rain? (Job 38:28)

*send lightning? (Psalm 144:6)

*make the oceans to boil like a pot? (Job 41:31)

*cause the trees to clap for joy? (Isaiah 55:12)

*scatter the east wind upon the earth? (Job 38:24)

*make mountains and hills break into singing? (Isaiah 55:12)

*set the stars in the sky and know their names? (Psalm 147:4)

*call forth fire out of a rock? (Judges 6:21)

*create the calendar? (Psalm 104:19)

*speak to the clouds and demand an abundance (Ezekiel 34:26) or no rain? (Isaiah 5:6)

*give peacocks goodly wings? (Job 39:13)

"How excellent is Thy loving-kindness, O God: I will praise Thee with my whole heart."
(Psalm 36:7)

We are scheduled to fly out Thursday morning, hopefully arriving in Fort Pierce around 4:00 PM. MFI does not keep Delta schedules.

Did you know that Haiti is a major transshipment point for South American narcotics, primarily cocaine, being sent to the United States?

Discover has missed us. I hope you did, too.

We will dawdle to reacclimate ourselves to the fast-paced American schedule by going to Daytona and St. Augustine to revisit some of their natural resources (premiere outlet malls) and let the beaches heal our feet. We plan to spoil ourselves anew with air-conditioning, Cracker Barrel, hot showers, smooth highways, telephones, fast Internet access, and ice cream. We should pull into Vale Drive on Monday.

Today we plan to walk to Milot to the west and to the villages to the east just to relish all that has happened here. It is beyond mere words to describe.

The people, Lord, we pray for the people.

We miss your dear faces and your spoken English, but God has blessed us in a whole new dimension.

Are the Haitians really that poor, or are the conditions there magnified? Well, the grammar school children here will soon be allowed to borrow shoes from Good Shepherd Ministry to use during school hours.

We could afford to live here.

Many of you have told me how moved you have been by the reality of Haiti. You ask me what you can do. Even these great GSM schools cannot change Haiti. Only God can. Please pray for the people.

Perhaps you have items you could send. In October they receive a container (the size of a truck) from America. This is the cheapest way to ship items here. They need building supplies for specific projects, household items, and classroom and sewing supplies: two yards or more of good fabrics—that piece you really do not like anymore, scissors, notions, computers, and computer paper. Items not shipped in the container cost $1.50 per pound to ship and space is at a premium. Include shipping funds if you can. You can send funds to:

Glen Iris Baptist Church Haiti Project
1137 10th Place South
Birmingham, Al 35205

If you want to donate items or funds, you can contact the American representative Lamar Lyon at lamar@gsmi-haiti.org and he will tell you what specific things they need and how to get them to GSM. All items are put to good use here.

One group of people put on a new roof. Another group is donating computers. The mission needs new iron beds for the groups that come here. Termites liked the wooden ones too much. I was told that Mercedes-Benz donates four-wheel-drive vehicles to third-world countries. If you know a contact there, this would satisfy a major need.

"The lips of the righteous feed many."
(Proverb 10:21)

Satan feels secure here, but he is a defeated foe. We have been promised that God will endure forever, and of His kingdom there shall be no end. (Luke 1:33)

We may have changed a lot since we left.

Physically: My arms look as if I have received a beating due to the red, purple, and yellow welts left by hungry gnats. These are not your typical American gnats. They replenish themselves daily with fresh blood to feed a new, vicious army, ready to attack.

Customs may quarantine me to be sure I do not have some horrible creeping skin disease.

I stayed physically fit with the necessary required unlimited hikes to my classroom and the bonus fitness test: the walk to the Citadel.

Jack has lost twenty pounds that he plans to leave here.

Mentally: How many Haitian dollars equals one American dollar? How many gourdes is that? What is a gourde? How many millimeters are in a yard and a half?

Emotionally: Picture my fifteen girls excited about class. I am tangled up in the hearts of these people.

Spiritually: How would *you* like to have almost unlimited time for Bible study?

Is God asking you to contribute items? Is He asking you to give your time and efforts? Is He asking you to pray?

Thank you for the many encouraging e-mails! Oh, that Job could have had friends like you! You have humbled and strengthened me with your interest and support. God's people listen when He speaks.

I won. I won.
Thank you, God

Lynda,
God's most grateful servant
Please be generous with your prayers.

48

Wednesday, April 08, 2009

They gave us a parade for leaving!
Not really.

A marching band came from Cap Haitien with donated drums, trumpets, uniforms—the whole works. This was a first for Haiti. They stopped in front of our gate to assemble for the march into Milot. They are celebrating King Christophe. That seems ironically close to the name of another King celebrated at Easter.

Haiti's first marching band

Joscelyn walked with me outside the gates and we visited as I made pictures. Later I saw a friend beckon to him to come, and he told his friend he could not—he had to protect me. I did not know until then that I had a guard.

We leave Bon Berger in the morning at 8:00 AM to catch a 10:00 AM MFI flight in Cap Haitien bound for Ft. Pierce, Florida, arriving late tomorrow afternoon.

I truly do not want to leave these people who have become so dear to me. The only thing that compels me to do so is remembering my family and all of you.

Please pray for these people.

Lynda,

Your Haitian refugee

(Yes, they do return refugees!)

49

Thursday, April 09, 2009

Leaving was emotional. The men in devotional had Joscelyn give a farewell speech to us, and it was touching. I do not cry attractively. We took a group photograph.

Packing is done. I am trying not to think about everything I am leaving.

People lined the street to see us off. It was so touching. I am sure it was a coincidence that there was another huge parade today on this main street in preparation for the weekend celebration of King Christophe.

This is my final slow drive down the highway from Milot to Cap Haitien. I watch out the window through tears, trying to memorize everything. The memory tape in my mind is busy both recording and playing back to me a flood of sweet memories.

The red berries that the vendors sometimes string into their coffee bean necklaces contain a poison as deadly as ricin toxin. The berries are grown here. There is no antidote. A person has four hours to three days if any gets into the bloodstream. We were warned by the medical team that customs was confiscating the necklaces, but the vendors are still selling them. I swapped mine for safe coffee bean necklaces. Bill negotiated the exchange for me.

The long drive is too short today. Bill left us at customs. It is 10:00 AM. He was not allowed to go past the glass security door.

Wait! I did not thank him for letting God use him here. Did I ever tell him how much this experience has strengthened my relationship with God? I cannot even see him now.

It is too late.

Now all these people are talking at us and we do not understand. I think this must be how a cat feels when you tell her something. Speaking loudly does not help.

Memories are already bubbling up in my mind.

There were three stations for check-in at the Cap Haitien International Airport. Each is the size of a small podium. The waiting room has eight rows of five seats. The one security scanner had about two feet of rollers before and after the scanner to place your items on for the ride through the scanner. There was no line.

MFI check-in counter and Jack

Would you fly over the ocean on an airline that, two months ago, had both of its planes broken? It is something to consider.

Our two handsome DC-3 pilots also served as flight attendants, luggage handlers, and cargo loaders. The pilot said his friends cannot believe that he gets to fly a DC-3 for a living. The right side of the plane was curtained off for the cargo. I could hear the soft meowing of a frightened cat in a pet carrier somewhere in that area. The left side of the plane held the double rows of passenger seats.

Lynda Criswell

The backs of our pilots' heads

Inside the DC3

This plane was built in 1943 and served in Africa. Do you think Rosie the Riveter worked on this plane? I would like to thank her. Thinking of the memories made in this plane is sobering.

By 11:00 AM we landed in Pignon, Haiti, on a dirt runway that was probably here when the DC-3 was new. Is that a goat on the runway? Yes, there is a goat tied by the runway. About twenty-five villagers came out to meet the plane. We took sixteen of them on as passengers. The missionaries are building wells here and have cut the typhoid rate by over fifty percent. Imagine worrying about typhoid.

Goat on the dirt runway at Pignon

One of the passengers had a blue jumper tarantula in a container to take home to Florida. I did not even stand by her.

We are now flying over endless typical barren Haitian landscapes with very few dirt roads, but still there are the isolated scattered huts. Most of Haiti is like this. Only the area around Milot and GSM supports more abundant plant life, but I saw very few tropical flowers even there. Haiti is about one-fourth the size of Alabama.

As we approach Port-au-Prince, we see relatively nicer homes. Some have concrete roofs; some have the weathered multi-colored tin roofs. But some have no roofs, too. Many rooftops are festive with clotheslines strung with colorful clothes drying.

The officials herded us into the airport at Port-au-Prince, and then walked away, stranding us. I guess they were not worried that one of us would make a break for it and escape into Haiti. People do not escape *into* Haiti.

It is about 12:30 PM.

Our pilot prays before taking off. When have you ever seen that happen? That is both reassuring and ominous. Where is my luggage that was tagged MIA ? Where is that tarantula? It is hot on this plane! My skin feels hot. Lunch is a foam cup of Diet Coke and an oatmeal snack cake, served by a passenger.

As the plane gained altitude, it became cold. It is cold on this plane! The snack several hours later was hot chocolate and another snack cake. Suddenly I am exhausted. I tried to sleep on the life preserver they gave me, but the plane was too noisy.

I wonder if decades ago a soldier on this same plane said exactly the same things.

I can see land below! There are highways, cars, yachts, many tall buildings, subdivisions named after whatever was destroyed to build them, lush green landscaped areas, and wide sandy beaches. I feel tears spring to my eyes.

Look! There is an American flag! There is our sweet car parked right under the flag! MFI has washed her. Thank you, God, for placing me in America!

Our flag. Our car

Customs at Fort Pierce did not take long. Even the tarantula made it through. We all just stood in a group until the pilots reminded us that we were free to go. We had forgotten what freedom means. This is our country. We were free to go home.

Customs official checking container for tarantula.

Customs looking for the tarantula

Jack cranked the car. It was so quiet we could not hear it. We drove away from MFI on a smooth, paved road with landscaping and curbs. No one seemed to notice us. We did not stand out. This is America! There are no United Nations trucks or helicopters watching us. We are free to drive away and go anywhere.

I see billboards and street signs and paved roads and traffic lights. Everyone is driving only on the right side of the road. Have you ever thanked God for paved roads? I see fat cows inside fences, not tied by the road. No one is staring at us and hollering "blanc".

We immediately tried to call our sons to tell them we were home, but Jack had literally forgotten how to use his complicated cell phone. I pulled my simple one out. We talked to Wes and Cara and Schaeffer and Cynthia and Jack—my wonderful family!

We drove thirty minutes before we stopped at a Dairy Queen. It was so cold inside. Why do Americans do that?

We are now at a Courtyard hotel (one of my personal favorites). Hot showers are only one of the many luxuries we are now enjoying again. The water has force. I can use my hair dryer. There is even a bathroom electrical socket. Did you know these rooms have big mirrors? And they have electricity all the time. What a good idea.

Tomorrow we explore the St. Augustine natural resources we mentioned earlier to see what the natives here have made.

Could I have dreamed Haiti? No, I still have swollen, discolored gnat bites. God has brought us back safely to America. God bless America.

So is this good-bye? You know me better than that!

Lynda,
Pray for the people

Father, thank You for Your patience and forgiveness toward me. Please remind me that the things in my life are just borrowed from You. You are the joygiver and the source of all true happiness.

50

Friday, April 10, 2009

I'm back!

Thank you for your overwhelming support and prayers that God used, and bless His word. He has abundantly answered your prayers.

I left a land of privilege, air-conditioning, and insurance willingly and eagerly to do God's will for me. God planned the whole journey. I recorded each experience as accurately as I could. If anything is incorrect, it is due to my misunderstanding. I went to a land of poverty. I loved the people with His love. I gave them His hope. I received a richer life. I regret leaving them, but this was part of His plan as well.

Isn't this what Jesus did on a much bigger, more perfect scale? He left His home of perfection willingly to come to our low level, loved us unconditionally, offered us lasting hope, and left us richer because that was God's plan.

This is a very poor comparison, of course. I did not suffer beyond gnat bites. I had no wisdom of my own to give them. I was the one enriched.

I learned that it is never a sacrifice to obey and follow God.

I learned that depending on God is an easy and rewarding thing.

I learned the overflowing joy of uninterrupted hours of fellowship from reading the Bible and praying.

I learned that the joy you receive from your children or from work is dull compared to what God offers, yet we spend more time developing the first relationships.

May I wish for you the same blessings God poured on me?

Here I am, Lord.
Is it I, Lord?
I have heard You calling in the night.
I will go, Lord,
If you lead me.
I will hold Your people in my heart.*

Lynda,

After today, a Haitian refugee

Please return the refugees.

Father, thank You for loving us enough to teach us what we need. Thank You for Your patience. Remind us that there is always more You want to give us, if we will just ask and receive it.

*Copyright Daniel L. Schutte. Used by permission.

51

Saturday, April 11, 2009

We woke up Friday morning in a temperature-controlled room facing a beautiful landscaped courtyard. We slept on high-count natural fiber linens and immensely enjoyed a luxurious hot shower with fragrant soap.

Outside the door was a morning paper. Remember those? I did not. I almost stepped on it. A *Wall Street Journal*! Professional landscaping! Who lives like this? Oh, yeah. We did.

I feel like an immigrant. Signs are fascinating; so are medical centers, car washes, grocery stores, car dealerships, department stores, sidewalks, and paved streets. Once, on the arduous journey to Cap Haitien when Bill was creeping over the pits in the road, a small child passed us on foot. I cannot believe I ever took culverts and curbs and water management and garbage pickup for granted.

Look! It is America! And she is beautiful. If you do not think God still has His presence and His people here, imagine living with voodoo parades and witch doctors. Thank you, God.

I stood in a convenience store at a gas station. People rushed all around me, not aware that emotionally I did not quite yet belong to their world. I saw Trident gum on the checkout display. Then I realized that I could buy that gum! I live in America!

We walked introspectively on Daytona Beach and let the wind comb our hair and the beach heal our feet. We quietly ate boiled shrimp and salad. We slowly walked Old St. Augustine and solemnly remembered God's blessings to us during the last two months. We sat in the quiet of Callaway Gardens. People around us ignored us. It is the American way.

I am awed when I look back at God's work in our lives. He arranged great jobs for Jack and me several times, and He removed them when His timing was right to open another door. There is no way we could have planned any of this.

Could you not say the same of your life? Do you wonder what He is planning for you now?

Lynda,
God's servant in Haiti and America
Soon to be back on Vale Drive

Father, I did what You told me to do. You have put Haiti and her wonderful people in my heart. You kept me in the cocoon of Your blessings every moment and fed me Your words. I do not want that to end. Remind me, Father, so that I please You always.

For God so loved the world, that He gave His only begotten Son, that whosoever believeth on Him should not perish, but have everlasting life. (John 3:16)

Appendix

Have you ever:

*seen non-perforated toilet paper? (Why would anyone make that?)

*seen an occupied house with a hard, dirt floor?

*seen an occupied house with no kitchen or bathroom?

*seen a dog too weak with hunger to move?

*seen a roach that … never mind.

*seen gnat bites that swell up to three inches in diameter and take literally days to heal?

*seen a row of beautiful Haitian girls, beaming and confident, and known every stitch in the garments they are wearing?

*seen the cook try to walk the model walk?

*seen how God desires to bless us, but we ask amiss?

*seen the excitement on a girl's face when she sees a garment go together that she designed and made?

*wished the one who donated the supplies could see that expression?

*cried when you cleaned a room because of the flood of good memories of the things that happened there?

*fixed your hair daily using a two-inch by two-inch mirror?

*lived with a bathroom that had no electrical outlets?

*communicated love to someone just by looking into their eyes when there was no common language?

*touched common fiberglass utility tables and metal chairs and machines and notions and thanked God for them?

*thanked God for those who generously supplied each of the above items?

*been overwhelmed with God's love just for you?

*noticed how beautiful all girls are?

*seen a girl's eyes dance with pleasure because she loved what God was teaching her?

*felt God's presence flood your soul with thanksgiving?

*asked God to bless a room to use for His glory and He did!

*out-given God?

*prayed that you would be usable to God, and He used you?

*stood in a silent, empty room and tried to absorb all the good things that happened there?

*actually absorbed the good things that happened there and did not want to leave?

*memorized a verse in another language and found it just as powerful?

*spoken to someone in his language, and he could not understand you?

*played count the lizards?

*worn the same three skirts (or pants) for eight weeks?

*run out of mouthwash and found your world did not end?

*paid no bills for eight weeks?

*read no newspaper and seen no television for eight weeks?

*knowingly stepped in stagnant water full of aging garbage while wearing sandals because there was no other choice?

*had a family of over ten people offer to share their two tomatoes and six sandwiches with you and your friends?

*wished for others to know the same deep contentment and pleasure you get from being in God's will?

*been awed to see God work?

*been surprised that God really did not need you to do His work? You need Him.

*noticed how odd it is that you do not terribly miss material things—only people. And maybe ice cream.

*panicked when you are on the last can of Baygon (like Raid) insecticide?

*been so blessed that you could not think of anything you could ask God for?

*awakened from a deep sleep to find you had scratched gnat bites until your arms were raw?

*taken America and her beauty and bounty for granted?

*been one of perhaps only one thousand people in your area to have a car?

*realized you could look at the sky and be as accurate as a meteorologist in forecasting rain?

*gone without food because you had none?

*been moved to tears by God's love?

*seen wonder, or possibly fear, in someone's eyes at a steam iron or a serger?

*found new joy in experiencing the truth in a familiar Bible verse again?

*been thankful that God wants to use you?

    I have.

    And I thank God for every second He has allowed me His blessings.

Would you like to know more?

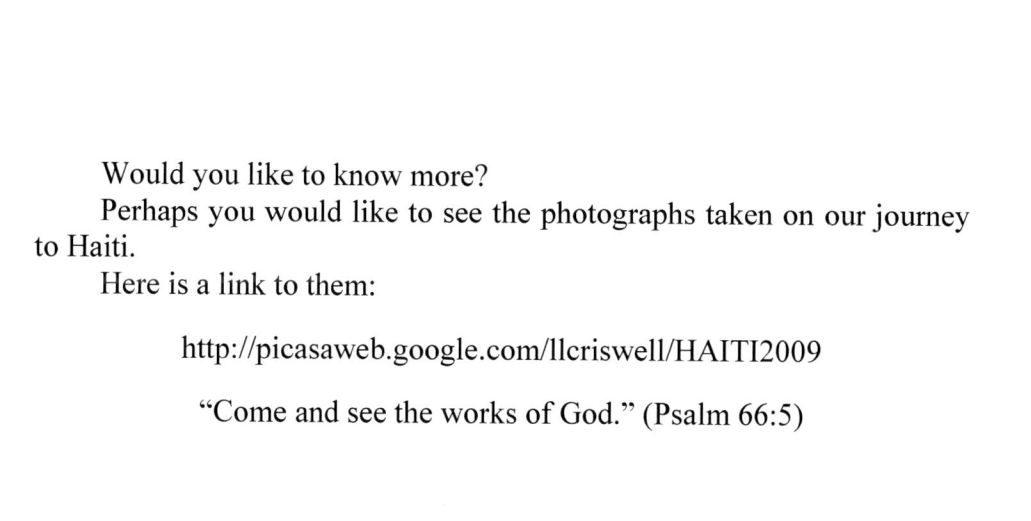

Perhaps you would like to see the photographs taken on our journey to Haiti.

Here is a link to them:

        http://picasaweb.google.com/llcriswell/HAITI2009

"Come and see the works of God." (Psalm 66:5)